# Oil & Vinegar

# Oil & Vinegar

EXPLORE THE ENDLESS USES FOR THESE VIBRANT
SEASONINGS IN OVER 75 DELICIOUS RECIPES

## WITH RECIPES BY URSULA FERRIGNO

Photography by JAN BALDWIN

RYLAND PETERS & SMALL
LONDON • NEW YORK

For Antonia, my little girl, whose passion for oil started at one-and-a-half and has continued to surprise me.

ISBN: 978-1-78879-069-7

10 9 8 7 6 5 4 3 2 1

Designers  Emily Breen and Toni Kay
Production controller  David Hearn
Art director  Leslie Harrington
Editorial director  Julia Charles
Publisher  Cindy Richards
Prop stylist  Jo Harris
Food stylist  Emma Marsden
Indexer  Hilary Bird

First published in 2019 by
Ryland Peters & Small
20–21 Jockey's Fields, London
WC1R 4BW
and 341 E 116th St
New York, NY 10029

www.rylandpeters.com

Recipes by Ursula Ferrrigno featured in this book were previously published by Ryland Peters and Small in The Gourmet Guide to Oil & Vinegar.

Text © Ursula Ferrigno 2014 , 2019 with the exception of pages 118–123 © Louise Pickford 2014, pages 116–117 © Valerie Aikman-Smith 2013 and pages 12–15 © Ryland Peters & Small 2019

Design and commissioned photographs © Ryland Peters & Small 2019. For full picture credits see page 144.

A CIP record for this book is available from the British Library.US Library of Congress cataloguing-in-publication data has been applied for.

Printed and bound in China

# Contents

# Introduction

When I announced to my family and friends that I was writing a book about oil and vinegar, I was surprised by their reaction, which was generally either 'is there enough to write about?' or 'aren't they just for salad dressings?' Oh how wrong can they be! Just as with any ingredient, the flavours in oils and vinegars must complement the foods they are paired with in order to bring out their subtleties. There are so many types of both these seasonings to choose from. Olive oil in particular (my personal passion) is highly prized and elegant bottles from Italy, France, Spain and now The New World are as beautiful to look at as they are to taste. As you cook and enjoy the recipes I have collected together here for the oil and vinegar aficionado, you'll discover which types of both these versatile seasonings I recommend for each of my dishes and learn how to use them instinctively in your own cooking. My influences are mostly Italian because of my own heritage so I've included many family favourites for you to enjoy – classic appetizers like Beef Carpaccio with Gorgonzola and Walnuts, refreshing salads, such as 'Dama Bianca', and exceptional pasta dishes, like Orecchiette with Chickpeas. You'll also learn how to make more delicate, refined dishes for entertaining, such as Poached Turbot with Watercress Oil and heartier aromatic meat dishes, including Pork Roast Braised with Milk and Fresh Herbs. I've included some Asian- and African-inspired recipes too, from Sweet Sticky Chinese Chicken to a Seven-vegetable Tagine. Why not put your baking skills to the test with moist, oil-drenched breads such as a Potato and Gorgonzola Focaccia before trying one of the sublime sweet treats on offer, from Italian Almond Apple Cake to a silky smooth Olive Oil Ice Cream, plus some deliciously novel vinegar-based sweet cocktails. Finally, you'll discover the secrets of multi-tasking marinades and salad dressings that you'll go back to again and again to add instant pizzazz to the simplest of dishes. Enjoy!

Oils

# Introducing oils

Oil is one of the most absorbing and tantalizing of subjects, as well as being exotic and romantic, because its origins are shrouded in mystery... Every olive oil producer I have met is truly passionate about this particular noble fruit and their dedication to producing and perfecting this historic food is often remarkable.

I love to use many different types of oil in my cooking but I have a personal passion for olive oil. This is undoutedly because some of my earliest memories in Italy are of my grandfather showing me precisely how to taste it. I enjoyed watching him smack his lips enthusiastically and closing his eyes if the oil he was trying was good.

Good olive oil is bountiful in the lands surrounding the Mediterranean Sea and many have access to excellent oil, which is often stored in large cans, carboys or demijohns and decanted into smaller bottles as needed. In Italy *La dispensa* (the storecupboard) is incomplete without these magical bottles filled with a golden or green elixir. The opportunity to smell and taste great oil as a child has stayed with me to this day. I think that there's nothing in the world that compares with a good, freshly milled olive oil.

There is evidence that olives were already being cultivated over 6,000 years ago. It is probable that the plant originated in Syria and it is thought to be very likely that the first people to transform the wild plant into a domestic crop spoke a Semetic language. The journey of olive cultivation from Syria to the Aegean Islands and the sunny hills of Anatolia was relatively straightforward. From there, it travelled on to the rest of Greece where it enjoyed unexpected success and was put to uses that made it indispensible to the ancient peoples of the Aegean. The use of olive oil in cooking then spread slowly westwards from the Eastern Mediterranean.

Olives would be harvested in September and October, and the timings are still the same to this day. Long poles were used to shake the branches and olives first tested for ripeness and quality by squeezing the juice from a few olives through a funnel into a small bottle. The flavour and smell of the oil extracted in this way was then evaluated, the precursor to the elegant bottles of olive oil we proudly display in our kitchens today.

But beyond my beloved olive oil we can now also use vegetable, canola, grapeseed, palm, peanut, avocado, sesame and coconut oils in our food, meaning that the world of culinary oil can be a very confusing place! For the best results with your cooking it's important to understand that when it comes to performance and flavour, not all culinary oils are created equal. Some perform well at high temperatures, making them ideal for frying/sautéing. Others are deliciously strong in flavour but turn rancid when heated so are best kept back for drizzling over a finished dish or as an ingredient in salad dressings.

In the pages that follow I profile types of olive oil and some of the most popular oils in use today – some long-established favourites, others that have recently gained in popularity due to their supposed health benefits. Use this information as a general guide in your own cooking and take your lead from the way in which I have used oils in my own recipes featured within this book, for example a delicious extra virgin olive oil for drizzling over simply grilled white fish, a toasted sesame oil in a tangy Asian-style dressing, a coconut oil to add an additional hint of flavour to spiced Indian dishes, a flavourless grapeseed oil for a mayonnaise, etc. Experimentation is key!

# Types of oil

As you will no doubt have noticed, a vast variety of different culinary oils are now available to buy. Buy the best you can afford and keep a good range to choose from in your kitchen as they serve myriad purposes – from using in simple salad dressings and marinades, to frying/sautéing and even in your baking.

## Olive oils

This magical oil is now an essential item in everyone's kitchen. There are hundreds of different varieties of olives, and styles of olive oil. Like grapes, the variety grown depends on the climate, the soil and also whether the olives are to be pressed for oil or preserved for eating. With table olives, the firmness and fleshiness of the fruit is of the greatest importance, whereas olives grown for pressing must have a high oil content. All olives are green at first and turn pinky, purpley and then black when fully ripe. Olives flourish in dry, arid conditions. The trees can survive long periods of drought but cannot tolerate extreme cold or damp weather, which is why olives are principally found in Mediterranean climes where the winters tend to be mild. That said, the 'New World' is experiencing a period of growth in its olive oil markets, with Chile, Argentina, South Africa, Australia, New Zealand and the USA at the forefront. South Africa is worth singling out as it has picked up many awards in recent years. Frying/sautéing with extra virgin olive oil is not recommended, as the heat causes the oil to burn and release free radicals. Also the flavour of the oil is often destroyed, along with the nutritional benefits. There are five grades of olive oil as designated by the International Olive Oil Council:

## Extra virgin olive oil

This is virgin olive oil of absolutely perfect taste and odour, having maximum acidity in terms of oleic acid of 1 g per 100 g or with an acidity of less than 1 per cent.

## Virgin olive oil

This is virgin oil of absolutely perfect taste and odour, but possessing a maximum acidity in terms of oleic acid of 1.5 g per 100 g or acidity of less than 1.5 per cent

## Olive oil

This is the oil mainly used to cook with. It is infact obtained from virgin olive oils by refining methods.

## Virgin olive oil lampante (lamp oil)

This is an off-tasting and off-smelling virgin pressing intended for refining or technical purposes.

## Olive residue oil

This is a crude oil obtained by treating olive residues with solvents and is intended for subsequent refining prior to human consumption.

## Almond oil

This is a pale, clean oil with a fairly neutral flavour and, rather surprisingly, not much of an almond taste. It is mainly used in baking and confectionery. It can be useful for oiling baking pans or soufflé dishes when making very delicately flavoured batters, or for oiling a marble slab when making sweets/candy. Used alone, it is not enough to give an almond flavour to cakes and biscuits/cookies. For that you need to use almond extract or, of course, almonds themselves.

### Argan oil

Argan oil comes from the fruit of the argan tree, native to the Argan forests of Morocco. It is green and fleshy, not unlike a ripe olive. The fleshy part is eaten by the nimble-footed goats who graze off the trees, digest the fleshy part and after nature takes its course the kernels are collected from the ground and pressed to yield a delicious and distinctive oil. It has a reddish tinge and nutty aroma. High in monounsaturated fats, essential fatty acids and antioxidants, it is used as a cooking oil in Morocco, to stir into couscous or add a final flourish to tagines. It makes a tasty dressing for salads and vegetables or can be mixed with ground almonds and honey to make a delicious spread for hot toast. It's costly as it takes 20 hours to render sufficient nuts to make 1 litre/quart of oil but a little goes a long way!

### Avocado oil

The oil of the avocado fruit has long been known for its properties as an ingredient in beauty products, but is now generating excitement in the health and fitness world as it is high in monounsaturated fats and cholesterol-free. It is one of the few fruit oils not derived from the seeds; it is infact pressed from the fleshy pulp surrounding the avocado stone/pit. Extra virgin avocado oil has the characteristically creamy flavour you would expect and an unbelievably high smoke point (250°C/482°F), making it a good choice for frying/sautéing but it really comes into its own when used in salad dressings. Look for 'Hass' cold-pressed avocado oil, which is emerald green – the colour is attributed to high levels of chlorophylls and carotenoids extracted into the oil. It has been described as having an avocado flavour, with grassy and buttery, mushroom-like notes. Because the avocado is a year-round crop, some olive oil processing facilities, particularly in Australia and New Zealand, process olive oil during the olive season, and avocado oil throughout the rest of the year.

### Coconut oil

Coconut oil is in high demand these days but the coconut has long been an important food source for people living in the tropical areas of Asia, Africa, the Pacific and South America. Pressed from the fruit of the coconut palm tree, coconut oil is ideal for light and subtly flavoured dishes. It gives a perfect hint of coconut flavour to Indian and South-east Asian recipes and works well in cakes and desserts. Choose from certified organic, either virgin (unrefined) or refined, depending on your needs and taste. Organic virgin coconut oil has a soft coconut aroma and more pronounced coconut flavour. If you are not keen on the taste or smell of coconut but you want the benefits of the oil, the organic refined version is a better choice. It stands up well to high heat and doesn't add any coconut flavour. Use organic refined coconut oil for sautéing and stir-frying. If you want to taste the coconut, perhaps in bakes, try virgin or extra-virgin, but take care as it can burn more quickly, making it better suited to medium to low-heat cooking.

## Corn/maize oil

This is one of the most economical and widely used of all edible oils. It is extracted from the germ of corn/maize. It is a deep, golden yellow with quite a strong flavour. Refined corn oil has a high smoke point making it a valuable all-purpose frying oil. It is technically suitable for all culinary uses including baking, but is not pleasant in salad dressings and mayonnaise.

## Citrus oils

These differ from other culinary oils in that they are used for flavour and not for emulsifying (as in mayonnaise), lubricating (as in salad dressings) or cooking (as in deep-frying). They are extracted from the essential oils stored in the skin of citrus fruits. Grapefruit, lemon and sweet orange oil are remarkable for their aroma and concentration. Just a drop is needed to permeate a dish with the scent and flavour of the fruit. Use them with a dash of gin or vodka to flavour a sauce for fish or chicken dishes. They are delicious stirred into custards or creams for cake filling but less successful added to cake batter since they are so volatile that they simply disappear.

## Grapeseed oil

A pale, delicate, quite neutral but pleasant-tasting oil, extracted from grape seeds, that is quite widely available. It is excellent for frying and for general culinary use, and it is a good choice for making mayonnaise. If you want to use hazelnut or sesame oil but find them too strong, then grapeseed oil is excellent for diluting them to your preferred concentration.

## Groundnut/peanut oil

This is a clear, pinkish-golden oil made by pressing specially-grown peanuts from Spain, China and India. It is also widely known as groundnut oil. The refined variety has been treated to mellow its strong peanut taste and create a mild-tasting oil with a thin pouring consistency that is suitable for frying and baking as well as in salad dressings and mayonnaise. It is used a great deal in French, South-east Asian and Chinese kitchens. It has a high smoke point and does not burn easily, making it a particularly good choice for wok cooking.

## Hazelnut oil

An expensive but delicious oil, this is one of the many nut oils that are now becoming more readily available. Use it on salads, with a little well-aged wine vinegar or lemon juice added, and maybe a few crushed hazelnuts. It is a richly flavoured, nutty brown oil that marries beautifully with fish, for example as a marinade and accompaniment for a raw fish salad. You could also, extravagantly, use it as the shortening when baking with ground hazelnuts. It works very well, but some of the flavour is lost when the oil is heated. However, it has such a powerful flavour to begin with that there is always more than enough left.

## Hemp/hempseed oil

Obtained by cold-pressing hemp seeds, unrefined hemp oil is dark to clear light green in colour with a nutty flavour. Although it is made from the cannabis flower, it should not be confused with hash oil. Rich in Omega-3, it is best used cold in salad dressings or to boost the nutritional benefits of in fruit smoothies and porridge bowls.

## Rapeseed/Canola oil

Bright yellow fields of rapeseed produce Britain's only home-grown source of edible oil. It was infact introduced as a crop by the Romans to provide oil, since olives would not grow in Britain. It is a bland, neutrally flavoured oil, suitable for frying, baking and general cookery. It is lower in saturated fats than most other commonly used oils. It is sometimes inaccurately called mustard oil because the rape plant, like mustard, is a member of the brassica family and confusingly has very similar yellow flowers.

### Sesame oil

Cold-pressed, unblended sesame oil has a rich, light brown colour, a distinctive smell and a strong, nutty flavour. Indeed, many people find it too strong and so a teaspoon mixed with a couple of tablespoons of delicate, flavourless grapeseed oil is sufficient. Sesame oil keeps extremely well, since it contains a substance that prevents it from going rancid. Toasted sesame oil, which has a deep golden colour, is an important ingredient in Japanese and Chinese cooking but it is more often used as a flavouring, seasoning or marinating ingredient than as a cooking medium, as the oil burns at a relatively low temperature. It is good used in dipping sauces for sushi or dim sum, for example.

### Macadamia oil

Macadamia nuts have grown in Australia's rainforests for thousands of years and were an important food for the Aboriginal tribes. But it took until the 1800s for botanists to discover their potential as a food crop. By this time, they had been transported to Hawaii, which subsequently became the world's largest commercial producer. However, in the 1960s, Australia finally started to grow the trees on a commercial basis and by 1995, production levels had overtaken those of America. Now, areas such as New Zealand, California, Israel and South Africa have also started production. The oil has a slightly sweet flavour. It has a high vitamin and mineral content, oozes with antioxidants, is cholesterol-free and has the highest levels of monounsaturated fats of all the nut and fruit oils, including olive oil. The nuts are sent to a processor and placed into drying bins. After drying, the nuts are cracked and the kernels separated from the shell; they are then mechanically pressed to extract the oil. Macadamia oil has a reasonably high smoke point, and works well in stir-fries, but its fine, buttery flavour is better suited to salads and salsas and to dress white fish and poultry after cooking.

### Sunflower oil

Sunflower oil is perhaps the best all-purpose oil. It is mild in flavour and pale yellow, also light in texture, which makes it excellent for frying and as an ingredient in baking but also in salad dressings and even as the base for mayonnaise, mixed with other more highly flavoured oils if desired. It is a good all-rounder and ideal for most every day cooking needs.

### Pumpkin seed oil

Pumpkins are only grown as an oil plant in a certain region of Central Europe: a small intersection comprising parts of Austria, Slovenia and Hungary – most of the oil currently comes from Styria, in South-east Austria. The oil is a dark, concentrated green colour and has a velvety texture and intense nutty flavour. It is high in monounsaturated fats, provides an ideal blend of omega-3 and omega-6 oils and is rich in many vital nutrients, including vitamins A and E, selenium and zinc. The seeds are coarsely ground, then toasted before the oil is extracted. It has a fairly low smoke point, so it's best reserved as a salad oil and to drizzle over cooked dishes. It makes a good alternative to butter on vegetables, and is good drizzled over soups and casseroles.

### Walnut oil

This flavourful nutty oil is made in France – in the Dordogne, Périgord and the Loire – and also in Italy. Production is small-scale, and it is therefore an expensive oil. It does not keep too well and once opened it should be stored in a cool place to prevent it from turning rancid. It is wonderful on salads, mixed with only a hint of a good raspberry vinegar or lemon juice. It also adds extra depth of flavour in baking. Try it in a walnut and coffee cake, in breakfast breads with a chopped walnut and raisin mixture, or to make walnut biscuits/cookies. You can also use it to flavour chicken sauces and marinades, and it is delicious drizzled over cooked French beans.

hazelnut oil

sesame oil

chilli-infused oil

sunflower oil

# Storing oils

Heat and light both have a degenerative effect on oils. Always buy them in dark glass bottles, cans or ceramic containers. Unlike many wines oils do not grow old gracefully, so do not buy them in bulk unless you use them in very high volume. Ideally, once a bottle of extra virgin olive oil or other high quality culinary oil has been opened, it should be used within 2–3 months.

You may sometimes see olive oil with a white solid layer at the bottom of the bottle. This happens when it has been exposed to the cold and will not damage or change the oil in any way. If a solid layer does form, simply return the oil to room temperature and it will recover. Nevertheless, it's always best not to store any oils for cooking in the refrigerator.

rapeseed/canola oil

walnut oil

groundnut/peanut oil

coconut oil

# Infused olive oil dressings

Good extra-virgin olive oil is delicious drizzled over salads and cooked dishes just as it comes, perhaps with a splash of aged balsamic vinegar or a squeeze of fresh lemon juice to add a little sharpness. It can however also be infused with herbs and other seasonings to create simple and elegant dressings that enhance rather than overwhelm the flavour of the oil and finish a range of dishes off to perfection.

## Lemon, olive and pepper

The oil is infused with lemon zest and slices, crushed olives and peppercorns for a few days, allowing the flavours to permeate the oil. The oil is then strained ready for vinegar or lemon juice to be added.

1 unwaxed lemon

8 large pitted green olives, sliced

½ teaspoon each black and pink peppercorns, bruised

150 ml/⅔ cup extra virgin olive oil

lemon juice, to taste

salt

MAKES 150 ML/⅔ CUP

Thinly pare the zest from the lemon and then, using a sharp knife, cut away the pith from the whole lemon. Cut the lemon into thin slices. Place the zest and slices in a sterilized jar with the olives and peppercorns (bashed slightly), pour over the oil and allow to infuse for 5 days.

Strain off and discard the flavourings and pour the oil into a bowl. Whisk in enough lemon juice for your taste and adjust seasoning to taste.

Drizzle over tomatoes or a tuna and bean salad.

## Bay and thyme

Bay and thyme give the oil a mellow flavour and, once strained, it is perfectly enhanced with a light vinegar, such as Chinese black vinegar or rice wine vinegar.

6 bay leaves

4 sprigs fresh thyme

salt and pepper

150 ml/⅔ cup extra virgin olive oil

1–2 tablespoons vinegar of your choice

MAKES 200 ML/ 1 SCANT CUP

Place the bay leaves, thyme, salt and pepper in a pestle and mortar and pound gently to bash up the herbs. Transfer to a jar, add the oil and marinate for 5 days.

Strain the oil into a sterilized jar, add vinegar, salt and pepper to taste and serve.

This dressing is great served over salad leaves or shaved courgettes/zucchini or even warmed mushrooms on toast.

# Smoked garlic oil

**8 tablespoons soft brown sugar**

**8 tablespoons long grain rice**

**8 tablespoons tea leaves**

**1 head garlic**

**250 ml/1 cup plus 1 tablespoon extra virgin olive**

**freshly squeezed lemon juice, to taste**

**salt and pepper**

MAKES 300 ML/1¼ CUPS

Tea-smoking is a terrific way to flavour foods. It is often used to smoke salmon or duck, but works well here with the garlic. You will need to double line the wok with foil and open a window when you are smoking foods as the aroma is quite pungent.

Line a wok with a double sheet of foil and combine the brown sugar, rice and tea leaves in the bottom. Place a small rack or griddle over the smoking mixture (making sure the two don't touch) and lay the garlic on the rack.

Place the wok over a high heat and, as soon as the mixture starts to smoke, top the wok with a tight-fitting lid. Lower the heat and cook gently for 15 minutes until the garlic turns a deep brown. Allow to cool.

Place the unpeeled garlic in a bottle or jar, add the oil and allow to infuse for 1 week. Drain and use the oil to make a dressing, adding vinegar or lemon juice to taste. Great with a beef carpaccio or a charred lamb salad.

# Saffron oil

The saffron adds both a pretty colour and a delightfully delicate flavour to the oil, which is delicious drizzled over grilled prawns/shrimp or a seafood risotto..

**a large pinch of saffron strands**

**1 tablespoon white wine vinegar**

**1 teaspoon caster/ superfine sugar**

**4 tablespoons extra virgin olive oil**

**salt and pepper**

MAKES 100 ML/⅓ CUP

Place the saffron, 1 tablespoon water, vinegar and sugar in a small saucepan and heat gently, stirring until the sugar is dissolved. Bring to the boil and remove from the heat. Set aside to cool completely.

Add the oil, season to taste and serve. Delicious with any grilled seafood or light rice dish.

# Basil oil

This oil is fragrant with pungent fresh basil leaves. It is best made in the summer months when basil is at its prime and, of course, most inexpensive.

**25 g/¾ oz. fresh basil leaves**

**300 ml/1¼ cup extra virgin olive oil**

**a little freshly squeezed lemon juice**

**a pinch of salt**

MAKES 100 ML/⅓ CUP

Whizz the basil leaves, oil and a little salt in a blender to make a vivid green paste. Allow to infuse overnight and the next day strain the oil through a layer of muslin/cheesecloth. Store the oil in the fridge, returning to room temperature before use.

This dressing is best served with lemon juice but, rather than mixing the juice into the oil, add it directly to the salad.

Arrange a plate of tomatoes and drizzle over some basil oil, squeeze with a little fresh lemon juice and serve.

# Vinegars

**THIS PAGE** Levizzano Castle in Castelvetro di Modena, Italy, and is one of the region of Modena's most famous landmarks. You may have come across the name Modena on your bottle of balsamic vinegar. It is the only area to produce it.

# Introducing vinegars

Vinegar is one of the oldest ingredients in cooking and was used in Europe for thousands of years before lemon juice was even heard of. The word vinegar originates from the French, vin aigre, meaning 'sour wine'. Today, a variety of alcohols are used as the basis of vinegars, not just wine.

Any alcoholic liquid that does not contain more than about 18% alcohol will sour if exposed to the air. Souring is caused by bacteria that attack alcohol and oxidize it to acetic acid. As they require oxygen, the bacteria grow on the surface and stick together to form a skin, known as 'vinegar plant' or 'mother of vinegar'. Vinegars normally contain 4–6% acetic acid, but the strength can be increased by distillation, and 'essence of vinegar' can be up to about 14%. Vinegar is commonly made by souring wine, beer or cider, but vinegars are produced locally from perry, mead, rice and wine, and from fruit wines brewed with anything to hand!

Wine vinegar is common in countries like France, Spain and Italy where wine is produced in quantity, but just because it is made from wine does not mean it is always good. It may be made from wine that is scarcely fit to drink, and it can be made using the quick vinegar process, in which wine is sprinkled over a container full of wood shavings with a revolving 'sparger', a miniature sprinkler. As the wine trickles down over the shavings, it is violently attacked by the organisms that cover them, and it is kept well oxygenated by air blown in at the bottom. In the process, heat is generated – the tank is maintained at 35–38°C (95–100°F), which is hot enough to drive off any of the finer and more volatile flavours.

This is why the best vinegar is still made using the old Orléans process, in which barrels are filled with a mixture of three parts wine to two parts vinegar, and inoculated with 'mother of vinegar' and left open to allow air to enter. Establishing the vat with vinegar encourages the development of vinegar organisms, which grow best in acidic conditions. In the Orléans process, the organisms slowly turn the alcohol in the wine to acid without getting hot and losing the finer flavours of the wine. At intervals, vinegar is drawn off and more wine is added. Since this is a slow method, Orléans process vinegar is expensive, especially as the finest vinegar starts with good wine. The town of Modena in northern Italy produces fine wine vinegar, aceto balsamico, which is matured for years. It is said that it is usable after 10 years, better after 30, better still after 50 and at its best after 100 or more!

Special types of vinegar come from particular wines, for example Sherry vinegar, which hails mainly from Jerez, Spain. Malt vinegar is essentially beer or ale vinegar (except that the beer is not hopped) and is coloured brown with caramel. It is less sour than a run-of-the-mill wine vinegar. Cider vinegar has long been popular in northeast America and in recent years in Britain as it is though to have health benefits. However, it has an apple juice taste that some people do not find that appealing. White vinegar is colourless (white wine vinegar, on the other hand, ranges from clear white to pale yellow) and is used in pickles for cosmetic reasons. It can be made by decolourizing vinegar with animal charcoal or can be faked by mixing acetic acid with water. Very strong concentrated vinegars, such as spirit vinegar and distilled vinegar, are used to pickle watery vegetables or in any other situation in which ordinary vinegar will become over-diluted and lose it's preserving properties.

# Types of vinegar

The range of vinegars available today is vast and the one you plump for will depend largely on your taste and what you plan on using the vinegar for. It is certainly worth experimenting with less common fruit and herb vinegars. When it comes to wine and balsamic vinegars, shop around, as the quality varies enormously. Discover how to make your own vinegar on page 30.

### Balsamic vinegar
Wonderfully dark and mellow, with a sweet-sour flavour, balsamic vinegar is made only in and around Modena in northern Italy (balsam simply means 'balm' and refers to the smooth, soothing character of the vinegar). There are two kinds: *industriale*, the commercial version, and *naturale*, which is still made by traditional methods in small quantities and aged for at least 15–20 years in wooden casks. There are reputed to be some exquisite vinegars that are well over 100 years old still in the possession of the families who produced them.

The vinegar is made from grape juice concentrated over a low flame and fermented slowly in a series of barrels, beginning with large chestnut or oak barrels and moving each year into progressively smaller barrels in a variety of different woods.

Balsamic vinegar is expensive, but a little goes a long way. Just a drop or two with some extra virgin olive oil makes a fine salad dressing. Do not mask the flavour with garlic and herbs or other flavours. Good mellow vinegars such as these can be surprisingly useful as a condiment to add to rich meaty soups or casseroles. Again, only a drop or two is needed. A classic dish from Modena is sliced strawberries simply sprinkled with a little balsamic vinegar and left to macerate for half an hour or so before serving.

### Cider vinegar
To make cider vinegar, pure apple juice is fermented into cider, which is then exposed to the air so that it sours and is thereby converted to acetic acid, in other words vinegar. It is a clear pale brown vinegar, although unpasteurized versions can be cloudy, and the apple taste is quite strong. It is suitable for salad dressings if you like the flavour, but I find it best of all for pickling fruit – pears and plums spiced with cloves and cinnamon sticks, and the cider vinegar sweetened with a dark sugar like molasses.

### Fruit vinegar
Raspberry vinegar, pear vinegar, blackcurrant vinegar, strawberry vinegar: the list of exotic new vinegars that have appeared in the last few years seems endless. However, they are not new at all. Look through any Victorian or even a much earlier cookery book and you will find a recipe for raspberry vinegar. Back then it tended to serve as the basis of a refreshing drink. Now it is used in salad dressings and particularly in sauces made from pan juices, for example when frying calves' liver or duck breasts. It also tastes very good when used as part of a basting mixture for roasting ham, duck or other fatty or rich meats.

Make fruit vinegar by steeping fresh fruit in wine vinegar and then straining it. For a more concentrated flavour, repeat this process with a second batch of fresh fruit in the same vinegar.

### Herb vinegar
Subtle yet distinctive flavours can be added to salad dressings by using red or white wine vinegar in which herbs have been steeped.

Tarragon vinegar is perhaps the most popular, but there is no limit to the herb-flavoured vinegars you can make. Basil vinegar, thyme vinegar, rosemary vinegar and lavender vinegar are ones I have used and enjoyed in salad dressings and in mayonnaise. Tarragon vinegar is particularly good in sauces based on eggs or butter, and is, indeed, an essential ingredient of sauce Béarnaise. It is important to use healthy, unblemished herbs, bought or picked at their peak of freshness. To make herb vinegars, simply steep a bunch of fresh herbs in wine vinegar in a sealed bottle.

## Malt vinegar

Just as wine vinegar is the everyday vinegar of wine-producing areas, and rice vinegar the everyday vinegar in those areas that produce rice wine, malt vinegar is commonly used in Britain and northern Europe, the 'beer belt'. It is made from soured, unhopped beer. In its natural form the vinegar is pale and usually sold as light malt vinegar. It may be coloured brown by the addition of caramel and will sometimes be called brown malt vinegar. In the same way that wine vinegars can be flavoured, so too can malt vinegar. It is common to find it flavoured with spices such as black and white peppercorns, allspice, cloves and tiny hot chillies/chiles. Often this is sold as pickling vinegar, since in the UK, it is malt vinegar that is usually used in the preparation of pickled onions, pickled walnuts and mixed vegetable pickles, such as piccalilli.

Use distilled malt vinegar to pickle particularly watery vegetables that are likely to dilute the vinegar. The vinegar is concentrated by distillation so that it has a higher proportion of acetic acid than the usual 4–6%. Distilled or white vinegar can also be made from other grains and is mostly used for pickling, though in Scotland it is used in the same way as ordinary malt vinegar.

On the whole, malt vinegars are best restricted to pickling and making preserves or bottled sauces such as tomato chutney. The malt flavour is too strong as a seasoning or for salad dressings. On the other hand, who could think of sprinkling wine vinegar on fish and chips? It has to be malt vinegar every time for that.

## Rice vinegar

Rice vinegar is made from soured and fermented rice wine. There are rice vinegars from China that are sharp and sour, and rice vinegars from Japan that are quite different: soft, mellow, rounded, almost sweet. Indeed, if you are planning to substitute a Western vinegar (cider vinegar is the best alternative) for Japanese rice vinegar in a Japanese dish, you will need to sweeten it a little. For a really authentic flavour in Asian cooking, when making seasoned rice for sushi for example, rice vinegar is essential. Always use Japanese rice vinegars with Japanese dishes, and Chinese rice vinegars with Chinese dishes. Fortunately, rice vinegar is also delicious in Western dishes, and

makes a perfect vinaigrette with, for example, a fine nut oil.

Like other vinegars, rice vinegars are sometimes made into flavoured vinegars: with soy sauce, dashi (Japanese soup stock) or mirin (a sweet rice wine for cooking) as the base, and then additions of grated ginger for shogazu vinegar, bonito flakes for togazu vinegar, toasted sesame seeds for gomazu vinegar and chillies/ chiles and onions for nanbanzu. Horseradish, mustard, citron and white radish (daikon) are also used to flavour it.

## Wine vinegar

Orléans in the Loire Valley, France, is the home of the wine vinegar industry, where the traditional lengthy fermentation processes are still followed (see page 25). Any vinegar made using the Orléans process, wherever it comes from, will be expensive but of superior quality. Wine vinegar – which is the strongest natural vinegar with an acidity of about 6.5% – is made from any wine untreated with preservatives. Not surprisingly, regions that are noted for a particular wine type also produce related vinegars. Among the more readily available wine vinegars are Champagne vinegar, which is pale, light and delicate; Rioja

balsamic vinegar

malt vinegar

cider vinegar

raspberry vinegar

vinegar, usually a red vinegar, which is rich, mellow and very full-bodied; and Sherry vinegar, a nutty brown vinegar matured in wooden barrels by methods similar to those used for sherry itself, and particularly full and rounded. All of these vinegars are of course especially suited to their local dishes, but are also excellent in all manner of salads. Interesting new wine vinegars are being made in other wine-making regions. For example, California produces a Zinfandel vinegar from the local grape variety.

The more expensive wine vinegars, such as Orléans vinegar and Sherry vinegar, are best used alone, but the more widely available red and white wine vinegars are the ones to use for experimenting with additional flavours.

Wine vinegars can be flavoured with fruit or herbs and also with honey, garlic, shallots, chillies/chiles, peppercorns, cloves, cinnamon, flower petals or even seaweed.

rosemary vinegar

red wine vinegar

white wine vinegar

Sherry vinegar

rice vinegar

# Making vinegars

Vinegar is very easily made at home by putting wine or any other alcoholic liquid into a container, preferably one with a tap/faucet at the bottom, and by adding 'mother of vinegar' (a fermenting bacteria composed of cellulose and acetic acid bacteria) to act as a 'starter' (a culture used to instigate souring). A skin of mother of vinegar will shortly form over the wine. If this later becomes too white and thick, the top layer should be removed, as it may prevent air from getting to the harmless bacteria beneath. The underlying pink skin should be left. When it is ready, some of the vinegar can be run off and more wine added. Vinegar exposed to the air will lose strength because of bacteria that attack the acetic acid, so vinegar bottles should be well filled and corked.

In the past, it was quite usual for cooks to make sugar vinegar, something that can be done quite simply as follows: boil a suitable volume of water and add sugar at the rate of 150 g/5½ oz. per 1 litre/quart. You can use brown sugar or add molasses for flavour. Traditionally, the liquid, when cool, was put in a not-quite-full cask and a piece of toast covered in yeast was floated on top. A piece of brown paper was pasted over the bung hole and well pricked with a skewer to let in air. A barrel of sugar and water, if put down in April, would be vinegar ready for bottling by September.

Old directions for making mother of vinegar are to put 100 g/3½ oz. sugar and 225 g/8 oz. treacle/molasses in 3.5 litres/quarts water and bring to the boil, then cool, cover and leave in a warm place for 6 weeks. If all goes well, mother of vinegar will form on top and can be used as a starter. Homemade vinegar is best pasteurized or brought almost to the boil before bottling.

Vinegar is often flavoured with various herbs and aromatics, the best-known varieties being tarragon, chilli/chile and garlic vinegars, but cucumber, basil, rose, violet, celery (with celery seed), cress or mustard (also with seed) and shallot vinegars are also made. To make any of these, it is necessary only to infuse the flavourings in a bottle of vinegar for some days. It used to be popular to make vinegars with quite complicated mixtures of herbs, garlic, onion and spices, which were essentially bottled sauces. Sweet fruit vinegars (such as raspberry, currant and gooseberry) were made for diluting and used in refreshing summer drinks, but these have also fallen out of fashion.

Due to its acetic acid content, vinegar is a preservative, which is why it is used in pickles and chutneys. As vinegars vary, it is sometimes best to dilute them with a little water and not to slavishly follow recipes with full-strength products. Tiny amounts of vinegar can improve some surprising things (yogurt and strawberries are examples).

Yamabukusu is a Japanese sweet vinegar, used for seasoning rice. You can quickly make your own version by adding 3 tablespoons sugar, 3 teaspoons salt and a pinch of monosodium glutamate to 250 ml/1 cup vinegar.

**THIS PAGE** Once you have mastered making your own vinegar, you can experiment with different flavours. Garlic, fresh red chilli/chile and tarragon are all perfect companions. It is worth making a wide range to use in different recipes.

# Herb vinegar

Occasionally we have some good red wine left over after dinner, and it really shouldn't be wasted. My Nonna was very frugal and was keen to teach the rest of the family to do the same. 'One day you will have a Ferrari if you are frugal enough!' she used to say. Here is a family recipe, which is a superb partner for the finest olive oil.

**500 ml/2 cups red wine**

**500 ml/2 cups white wine vinegar**

**2–3 garlic cloves, peeled and cut**

**3 sprigs fresh thyme**

**3 sprigs fresh rosemary**

**3 sprigs fresh oregano**

**8–10 peppercorns, crushed**

MAKES 1 LITRE/4 CUPS

Mix the red and white wine vinegar together. Add all of the other ingredients. Pour it all into a bottle and seal. Put it away for at least 1 month. You will have the most deliciously flavoured wine vinegar.

# Chocolate balsamic vinegar

Serve with ice cream, salads, and even steak. You will be surprised.

**50 ml/3 tablespoons cider vinegar**

**50 ml/3 tablespoons balsamic vinegar**

**50 g/2 oz. dark/bittersweet chocolate (minimum 70 % cocoa**

**solids), finely grated**

**75 g/scant ½ cup soft brown sugar**

MAKES 150ML//¾ CUP

In a medium-sized saucepan, gently heat the vinegars and sugar. Stir until the sugar has dissolved. Slowly bring to the boil and allow to boil for 5 minutes. Remove the pan from the heat, whisk in the chocolate and leave to cool. Decant into a sterilized jar when cold.

# Raspberry vinegar

Easy, stunning, versatile and so, so colourful. Please have a go. Make it for family and friends as a gift. Once you have tried it, you may like to try a gooseberry and lemon balm version.

**500 g/4 scant cups raspberries**

**300 ml/1¼ cups cider vinegar**

**175 g/¾ cup sugar**

MAKES 500 ML/2 CUPS

Crush the berries with a fork in a large glass bowl and pour over the vinegar. Cover and leave for 4 days, stirring once or twice.

Carefully strain through muslin/cheesecloth (don't crush the fruit or the vinegar will turn cloudy). You should have approximately 500 ml/2 cups of liquid.

Boil the raspberry liquid with the sugar very gently until the sugar has dissolved. Pour it into warm, sterilized jars. The vinegar will keep for a year. Great news!

# Recipes

# SALADS AND SOUPS

## Tomato and mint salad

I remember this salad from a business trip in Sicily where family friends were kind enough to serve it for lunch. The taste of the salad reflects the region's Byzantine flavour, typified by the mint, which releases a special flavour when blended with red onions. Be discerning when choosing tomatoes. I often find cherry tomatoes on the vine have a reliably good flavour compared to other varieties. Buy them when they're firm and bright in colour. In Italy, Spain and France you can buy your tomatoes in so many different degrees of ripeness. You will often be asked if you want to eat them that day, the next day or use them to make a sauce. I really enjoy being allowed to choose the different tomatoes. To pick the best ones, smell the stalk end – they should smell peppery.

4 firm, bright red tomatoes

½ a small red onion

a handful of fresh mint leaves

sea salt and freshly ground black pepper

2 tablespoons fruity extra virgin olive oil

1 tablespoon balsamic vinegar

25 g/1 oz. freshly grated Parmesan shavings

TO SERVE:

crusty or French bread

SERVES 4

Cut the tomatoes into slices. Peel and slice the onion into fine rings.

Arrange the sliced tomatoes and onions on a serving plate before adding the mint leaves.

Season to taste with salt and pepper, then pour over the olive oil and balsamic vinegar. Sprinkle the Parmesan shavings over the top and serve with bread.

# Pickled cauliflower salad

1 medium cauliflower

fresh bay leaves (optional)

55 g/½ cup green olives, halved and stoned/pitted

1 tablespoon good-quality capers

2 tablespoons sundried tomatoes, drained of oil and chopped

1 roasted red (bell) pepper, chopped into fork-friendly pieces

a handful of flat-leaf parsley leaves, finely chopped

2 tablespoons fresh and fruity olive oil (preferably Sicilian)

2 tablespoons red wine vinegar

sea salt and freshly ground black pepper

SERVES 4

Cauliflowers are at their best in the winter in Italy. Olives, too, will have just been harvested and will be used for the first time at the Christmas table. As a diehard cauliflower fan, I am so thrilled with the renaissance that cauliflower is experiencing. One great tip I've learned is that adding fresh bay leaves while cooking cauliflower dissipates the smell.

Cut the cauliflower into small, uniform-sized florets. Rinse well in cold water and drain. Put the florets and bay leaves (if using) in a large saucepan and add cold water to cover. Add 1 teaspoon of salt and bring to the boil. Boil for 3 minutes, then drain and refresh in cold water and discard the bay leaves.

Meanwhile, in a salad bowl, combine the olives, capers, sundried tomatoes, roasted red (bell) pepper, parsley and seasoning, then mix in the cauliflower.

In a small bowl, whisk together the oil and vinegar. Add to the vegetables and stir. Cover and leave for 1 hour before serving.

# Pantelleria potato salad

6 waxy new potatoes, peeled

3 tablespoons extra virgin olive oil

1 tablespoon red wine vinegar

1 tablespoon capers, rinsed if they are salted

8 small ripe tomatoes, cut in half

8 pitted/stone black olives

1 small red onion, cut into thin semicircles

a pinch of dried oregano

sea salt and freshly ground black pepper

SERVES 4

I had read about the Sicilian love of potatoes. The rich volcanic soil is the reason that the island produces such excellent potatoes. On a visit I was amazed to see so many varieties piled high on carts along the roadside, and by the quantities that people bought. This delicious salad is the perfect way to enjoy new potatoes in summer.

Boil the potatoes until tender – the time this takes depends on the variety and size. Drain and leave to cool. Cut in half if large.

In a large bowl, whisk together the oil and vinegar and toss in the remaining ingredients. Add the potatoes, toss to coat and season well with salt and pepper. Transfer to a serving dish.

# Fennel and celery salad

2 medium fennel bulbs,
stalks cut off and discarded

6 pale inner celery stalks/ribs,
leaves discarded and thinly sliced

250-g/8-oz. ball fresh buffalo
mozzarella, torn into chunks

½ tablespoon finely grated lemon
zest (preferably from an unwaxed
organic lemon)

2 tablespoons freshly squeezed
lemon juice

6 tablespoons fruity extra virgin
olive oil

¼ teaspoon fine sea salt

SERVES 6

The inner stalks of celery and fennel, plus creamy
and moist chunks of buffalo mozzarella create
a clean, cool and striking salad. The Italian name
for the dish – Dama Bianca – which refers to
a 'woman in white', alludes to its pale hues.

Halve the fennel lengthways, then thinly slice crosswise about
½ cm/¼ in. thick. Toss with the celery and arrange on a serving
platter with the torn mozzarella.

Whisk together the lemon zest, juice, oil and sea salt. Drizzle
the dressing over the salad just before serving.

# Broad bean and pea salad with sourdough croutons and tarragon

250 g/9 oz. podded broad/fava beans

200 g/7 oz. peas (ideally podded fresh garden peas if available)

3 slices of sourdough bread, ideally a little dry

1–2 tablespoons olive oil

4 tablespoons crème fraîche or sour cream

2 teaspoons Dijon mustard

finely grated zest and juice of 1 unwaxed organic lemon

1 garlic clove, crushed

sea salt and freshly ground black pepper, to taste

100 ml/6 tablespoons fruity extra virgin olive oil, plus extra for drizzling

40 g/⅓ cup freshly grated Parmesan cheese, plus extra shavings for scattering

2 generous handfuls of fresh tarragon, chopped, plus extra leaves for scattering

2 Little Gem lettuces or several handfuls of Cos/Romaine lettuce

SERVES 4–6

This salad is full of summer promise and is made all the better if the vegetables come from your garden. It is one of my favourites. Why not make your own bread to serve alongside it?

Bring the water to the boil in a medium-sized saucepan. Add some salt and the beans and cook them for 5 minutes. Refresh the beans with cold water, drain them well and remove the skins to reveal their vibrant green flesh.

If the peas are young and sweet, they can be served raw. If not, cook them for 3 minutes in boiling water, then refresh in cold water to prevent them cooking further.

Cut the bread into fork-friendly squares and heat the olive oil in a frying pan/skillet. Fry until golden, then put aside.

In a small bowl, combine the crème fraîche or sour cream with the mustard, lemon zest and juice and garlic, season with salt and pepper and slowly add the extra virgin olive oil until you have a thick, dressing. Add the grated Parmesan cheese. The thickness of the dressing should be that of double/heavy cream. Add water to slacken it if necessary. Add the chopped tarragon to the dressing.

Tear the lettuce and toss into a serving bowl with the beans and peas. Pour over the dressing and add half of the croutons. Toss to mix. Scatter with the remaining croutons, tarragon leaves and Parmesan shavings.

Drizzle the salad with a little more of the extra virgin olive oil just before serving.

# Pea shoot, endive, Provolone, pear and walnut salad

Provolone is a cow's milk cheese from Italy's southern region. It has a slightly smoky flavour and fine texture. The colour is pale yellow when aged between 2 and 3 months, but as the cheese ripens, the colour and flavour deepen. A mature goat's cheese would also work very well.

**100 g/1 cup fresh walnut halves**

**1 head chicory/Belgian endive**

**½ head radicchio**

**a handful of fresh basil leaves, torn**

**a handful of mint leaves, chopped**

**125 g/4½ oz. pea shoots**

**2 large, ripe but firm pears (Williams are good)**

**150 g/5½ oz. Provolone cheese, cut into triangles**

**FOR THE VINAIGRETTE:**

**¼ teaspoon fine sea salt**

**1 tablespoon red wine vinegar**

**2 teaspoons aged balsamic vinegar**

**3 tablespoons walnut oil**

**1 tablespoon olive oil**

**freshly ground black pepper, to taste**

SERVES 4–6

Preheat the oven to 180°C (350°F) Gas 4.

Spread the walnut halves out on a baking sheet and bake them for 10 minutes until they are fragrant. Let cool before roughly chopping.

Next, make the vinaigrette. Combine the salt, red wine vinegar and balsamic vinegar in a bowl and whisk until the salt has dissolved. Trickle in the two types of oil, whisking all the while until the mixture has emulsified. Season to taste with pepper.

Separate the chicory/endive and radicchio leaves, rinse well and pat dry. Place in a bowl with the herbs and pea shoots. Add 2 tablespoons of the vinaigrette and toss well, then transfer to a serving platter.

Quarter and core the pears, then arrange them on top of the bed of leaves and scatter over the cheese and walnuts. Drizzle with the remaining dressing and serve straight away.

# Asian-style carrot salad with ginger dressing and pumpkin seeds

**30 g/¼ cup pumpkin seeds**

**6 tablespoons tamari sauce**

**4 medium carrots, cut into matchsticks**

**150 g/5½ oz. pea shoots**

**3 spring onions/scallions, sliced at an angle**

**FOR THE GINGER DRESSING:**

**1-cm/½-in. piece of fresh ginger, peeled and grated**

**2 tablespoons mirin (sweetened rice wine)**

**1 tablespoon rice vinegar**

**2 tablespoons toasted sesame oil**

**sea salt and freshly ground black pepper, to taste**

SERVES 4–6

This salad is full of history for me. As a very young cookery teacher, I used to demonstrate this dish regularly. I love its colours and crunch factor. Providing your storecupboard is well stocked, this salad can be made quickly with easily.

Dry-fry the pumpkin seeds (without any oil) in a medium-sized frying pan/skillet and constantly toss the pan to prevent the seeds from burning. Once they start to colour, turn off the heat, add 4 tablespoons of the tamari and stir to combine. Leave them to cool and go crunchy.

Now make the dressing. Combine the ingredients in a jam jar with a screwtop lid. Season with salt and pepper. Shake to combine and set aside until needed. The dressing will store very well in the fridge.

Combine the carrots, pea shoots and spring onions/scallions. Sprinkle over the crunchy pumpkin seeds. Shake the dressing to mix, pour it over the salad and serve at once.

# Farro and bean soup

Barley-like and light brown in colour, farro has recently been rediscovered and is now valued both for its taste and nutritional value. Farro is cultivated almost exclusively in the Garfagnana, the mountainous region of Tuscany, and its use has brought a fresh recognition to Tuscan cooking. This soup is typical of Garfagnana.

**250 g/9 oz. dried borlotti beans, soaked overnight, drained and rinsed**

**2 medium white onions, finely chopped**

**5 fresh sage leaves**

**3 garlic cloves**

**4 tablespoons/¼ cup olive oil**

**1 medium red onion, finely chopped**

**2 carrots, diced**

**2–4 celery sticks/ribs, diced**

**a handful of fresh flat-leaf parsley**

**275 g/9½ oz. canned Italian plum tomatoes and their juice**

**200 g/1¼ cups farro, soaked overnight, drained and rinsed**

**sea salt and freshly ground black pepper, to taste**

**6 tablespoons estate-bottled extra virgin olive oil**

SERVES 8

Place the beans in a large saucepan with one onion, half the sage, one of the garlic cloves and enough water to cover by at least 5 cm/2 in. Cover and cook for 1 hour or until tender. When the beans are cooked, pass the contents of the pan through either a food processor or a vegetable mill.

Heat the oil in a large saucepan. Add the red onion and remaining white onion, the carrots, celery, most of the parsley, remaining garlic and sage leaves, the tomatoes and 3 tablespoons hot water and continue to cook for 10 minutes.

Add the farro and simmer on a low heat for around 30 minutes until tender. Add the bean mixture and then salt and pepper to taste. Stir and warm through until hot. Taste and adjust the seasoning, if necessary.

Ladle into serving bowls, drizzle with the extra virgin olive oil and finish with scattered leaves from the remaining parsley.

# Leek and tomato soup with crusty bread and basil

I am hungrily eyeing the leeks growing at the moment in my garden. Picking them young and tender is the secret to this totally memorable soup. I love the mixture of the humblest of ingredients married together, relying on an exceptional oil for a total taste sensation.

**6 baby leeks**

**3 tablespoons olive oil**

**750 g/1 lb. 10 oz. fresh, ripe tomatoes**

**sea salt and freshly ground black pepper, to taste**

**½ teaspoon crushed dried peperoncini chillies/chiles**

**450 g/1 lb. crusty day-old bread**

**750 ml/3 cups good vegetable stock**

**6 fresh basil leaves**

**12 teaspoons extra virgin olive oil**

SERVES 6

Slice the leeks and wash them well under cold running water.

Heat the olive oil in a large saucepan and add the leeks. Fry/sauté them for 10 minutes.

Purée the tomatoes in a blender or food processor and add them to the leeks. Add salt and pepper to taste, together with the peperoncini chillies/chiles. Simmer, uncovered, for about 30 minutes.

Cut the bread into small pieces and add it to the pan. Combine well, and lightly cook for 5 minutes. Add the stock, mix well and simmer, uncovered, for a further 10 minutes.

Ladle into serving bowls. Add a basil leaf and swirl 2 teaspoons extra virgin olive oil to each serving.

# FISH

## Mackerel with apple, watercress and ajo blanco

6 fresh mackerel fillets, skin scored diagonally at finger-width intervals

1 tablespoon olive oil

freshly squeezed juice of 1 lemon

3 medium-sized crisp, sweet apples, cored and sliced

150 g/5½ oz. watercress

2 tablespoons red wine vinegar

1 small red onion, very finely sliced for garnish

sea salt and freshly ground black pepper, to taste

**FOR THE AJO BLANCO:**

50 g/1¾ oz. stale white bread, crusts removed (sourdough is best)

125 g/1 cup blanched white almonds

1 garlic clove, chopped

1 tablespoon white balsamic vinegar

2 tablespoons Spanish extra virgin olive oil

SERVES 6

This is a fine combination of flavours. I first demonstrated this recipe at a farm called Burwash Manor, near Cambridge, England. It was their annual Apple Day and the response was very encouraging indeed!

Start by making the ajo blanco. Soak the bread in a bowl with cold water for 15 minutes. Meanwhile, finely grind the almonds in a food processor. Pour in 100 ml/scant ½ cup of cold water and combine to blend until you have a loose paste. Add the garlic and blend. Drain the bread and add it to the almond paste, along with the vinegar and extra virgin olive oil. Transfer to a bowl and season to taste. Cover and transfer to the fridge for at least 1 hour.

Heat a griddle/grill pan until hot. Brush the mackerel with the oil and season well with salt and pepper. Cook in the hot pan for 4 minutes, skin-side down. Turn and cook for a further 2 minutes. Squeeze the lemon juice over the fillets.

Mix the apples, watercress and red wine vinegar together and divide between serving plates. Top with the warm mackerel, a dollop of ajo blanco and garnish with slices of red onion. Serve immediately.

# Pickled lox

300 ml/1¼ cups distilled white vinegar

125 g/⅔ cup light brown sugar

25 g/2 tablespoons sea salt

6 fresh bay leaves

2 teaspoons coriander seeds

2 teaspoons yellow mustard seeds

1 teaspoon black peppercorns

1 teaspoon allspice berries

20 g/a handful of fresh dill, chopped, plus extra to garnish

500-g/1-lb. salmon fillet, skin on

1 white onion, finely chopped (optional)

TO SERVE:

rye bread

cream cheese

SERVES 8

This recipe is in honour of my friends in Ukraine. The chefs that I have worked with over there are very proud of their national dishes and my recipe is inspired by one I have enjoyed. I hope you will return to frequently for its ease, flavour and wow factor. Be aware that the pickling takes time so you need to start work 3 days ahead of when you plan to serve the dish.

Put all the ingredients except the salmon and onion into a non-reactive saucepan with 1 litre/1 quart water and bring to the boil. Turn down the heat and simmer for 5 minutes. Remove from the heat and leave the brine to cool to room temperature in the pan.

Put the salmon fillet in a non-reactive container and pour over the brine. Cover lightly. Put into the fridge and leave for 3 days.

Take out the salmon out of the brine (reserving the liquid) and cut into very thin slices, removing and discarding the skin as you go. Put the slices in a shallow bowl with the chopped onion, if using, and about 100 ml/½ cup of the reserved brine.

Serve on slices of rye bread that have been spread liberally with cream cheese and garnish with dill.

# Poached turbot with watercress oil

6 fillets of turbot, about 190 g/
6½ oz. each, skinned

**FOR THE COURT BOUILLON:**

1 carrot

1 stick/rib of celery, sliced

1 small onion, sliced

2 teaspoons fine sea salt

1 teaspoon black peppercorns

a handful of fresh flat-leaf parsley

200 ml/¾ cup dry Vermouth

**FOR THE WATERCRESS OIL:**

2 tablespoons rock salt

150 g/15½ oz. watercress,
plus extra to garnish

120 ml/½ cup extra virgin rapeseed/
canola oil

3 tablespoons extra virgin olive oil,
not peppery or heavy but appley/
green

3 teaspoons freshly squeezed
lime juice

sea salt and freshly ground
black pepper, to taste

SERVES 6

Turbot is a treat and is certainly one to reserve for special occasions. The watercress oil is a perfect companion for this oh-so delicious fish.

Place the ingredients for the court bouillon in a saucepan with 1.4 litres/6 cups water and bring to the boil. Turn down the heat and simmer, uncovered, for 30 minutes. Strain the vegetables through a sieve/strainer into a roasting pan. Discard the vegetables and set the pan of bouillon to one side until needed.

Have a bowl of iced water ready for the watercress oil. Fill a saucepan with water and add the rock salt. Bring to the boil and add the watercress. Blanch for 25 seconds, then drain and immediately immerse in the bowl of cold water. Drain the watercress and squeeze out as much moisture as possible. Pat dry with paper towels and roughly chop. Place the watercress in a blender or food processor with a little salt and pepper and half of the rapeseed/canola oil, and blend for 20 seconds. With the motor running slowly, add the remaining rapeseed/canola oil, the extra virgin olive oil and lime juice. Season to taste and set aside.

For the turbot, bring the court bouillon in the roasting pan to a gentle simmer on the hob/stovetop. Carefully place the turbot fillets in the hot liquid and poach for 8–12 minutes until the fillets turn opaque. The cooking time will depend on the thickness of the fillets. Do not allow the liquid to boil. Lift out the fillets and place them on a warm plate with watercress to garnish and finish with a drizzle of the watercress oil. Serve immediately.

# Black cod with olives and potatoes in parchment

A favourite that originated in the Italian port of Bari (often named after San Nicola, the guardian saint of sailors), these little packets seal in the fish and vegetable juices, with the potato slices insulating the fish from the heat of the oven. The olives and lemon slices emphasize the bright flavours of the dish.

250 g/9 oz. small new potatoes

3 tablespoons plus 1 teaspoon olive oil

1 tablespoon plus 2 teaspoons fresh oregano leaves, finely chopped

2¼ teaspoons fine sea salt

8 x 150-g/5½-oz. pieces skinless black cod, Pacific cod or haddock fillet (about 2.5 cm/1 in. thick), any bones removed

1 unwaxed organic lemon, very thinly sliced

6 garlic cloves, peeled and thinly sliced

125 g/1 cup Kalamata black olives, pitted and cut into slivers

a handful of fresh flat-leaf parsley leaves, chopped

delicate extra virgin olive oil for drizzling

an adjustable blade slicer, 27.5–37.5 cm/11–15 in. (optional)

baking parchment

kitchen twine

SERVES 8

Preheat the oven to 200°C (400°F) Gas 6, with a baking sheet on the bottom shelf/rack.

Cut the potatoes into very thin slices using the blad slicer or a sharp knife. Toss the slices with 2 tablespoons of the oil, 1 teaspoon oregano and ¼ teaspoon sea salt. Divide the potatoes among 8 large squares of parchment, arranging them in the centre so that they overlap slightly, then top with a fish fillet. Sprinkle each fillet with a scant ¼ teaspoon sea salt, then top each with a lemon slice, a few garlic and black olive slivers, parsley, ½ teaspoon oregano and ½ teaspoon olive oil.

Gather the sides of the parchment up and over the fish to form a pouch, leaving no openings, and tie tightly with kitchen twine. Put the packages on the hot baking sheet and bake until the fish is just cooked through, 15–22 minutes.

Cut open the parchment parcels to serve and drizzle with the extra virgin olive oil.

Cook's note: The fish can be assembled in parchment 4 hours ahead and kept chilled.

# Sicilian-style tuna with fennel and chillies

**FOR THE MARINADE:**

125 ml/½ cup Sicilian extra virgin olive oil

4 fresh red chillies/chiles, deseeded and finely chopped

4 garlic cloves, crushed

grated zest and freshly squeezed juice of 3 unwaxed lemons

a large handful of fresh flat-leaf parsley, finely chopped

sea salt and freshly ground black pepper, to taste

**FOR THE TUNA:**

4 x 125-g/4-oz. tuna steaks

2 fennel bulbs, finely sliced through the root

2 red onions, finely sliced

2–3 tablespoons olive oil

**TO SERVE:**

crusty bread

SERVES 4

My lasting memories of Sicily are travelling on a business trip with my father. Business was conducted not in an office restaurant but in a fish market, then in the car, and then in the kitchen where this dish was prepared for us. I shall never forget this lunch. I experienced such convivial hospitality and memorable food that I have now written about it in two books.

For the marinade, mix all the ingredients together in a bowl and season to taste.

Place the tuna steaks in a shallow dish and cover with 2–3 spoonfuls of the marinade. Reserve the remaining marinade.

Place a griddle/grill pan or frying pan/skillet over a medium heat. Toss the fennel and onions with the oil, then cook for 5 minutes on each side to soften. Place on a plate and drizzle with the reserved marinade.

Fry/sauté the tuna steaks in the griddle/grill pan or frying pan/skillet until cooked to your liking, approximately 4–5 minutes on each side.

Serve the tuna steaks on the vegetables with some crusty bread on the side to soak up the juices.

# Swordfish skewers with walnut sauce

1 kg/2¼ lbs. swordfish, skin removed and cut into 2 cm/¾ in. cubes

grated zest and freshly squeezed juice of 2 unwaxed organic lemons

175 ml/¾ cup olive oil

a handful of fresh mint leaves, finely chopped

large handful of fresh bay leaves

2 unwaxed lemons, cut into wedges

sea salt and freshly ground black pepper, to taste

**FOR THE WALNUT SAUCE:**

125 g/1¼ cups fresh walnut halves

1 large garlic clove

160 ml/⅔ cup walnut oil

1 slice of white or brown sourdough, soaked in water

freshly squeezed juice of 1 lemon

sea salt and freshly ground black pepper, to taste

6 wooden skewers, presoaked in water to avoid them catching and burning

SERVES 6

Any firm white fish works well here and the skewers can be cooked under the grill/broiler or on the barbecue or over a charcoal grill in summer.

Put the fish cubes, lemon zest and juice, olive oil, mint, salt and pepper in a large bowl. Toss the fish to coat, cover and leave in the fridge for a minimum of 1 hour.

Meanwhile, make the walnut sauce. Preheat the oven to 200°C (400°F) Gas 6, and line a baking sheet with baking parchment. Toast the walnuts on the lined baking sheet for 8 minutes.

Blend the walnuts in a food processor with the garlic, walnut oil, bread (squeezed dry) and the freshly squeezed lemon juice, scraping down the sides as necessary. You should have a thick, smooth sauce. Season to taste.

Remove the fish from the marinade and reserve the liquid. Thread the cubes onto skewers, alternating with bay leaves and lemon wedges.

Preheat a grill/broiler to medium and cook the skewers, turning after 10 minutes and brushing with the reserved marinade. Alternatively, cook on a hot barbecue/gas or charcoal grill for 6 minutes, brushing with the marinade.

Serve the skewers with the walnut sauce on the side.

# MEAT AND POULTRY

## Carpaccio with Gorgonzola and walnuts

750-g/1 lb. 10-oz. beef fillet,
tail end in one piece

200 g/7 oz. rocket/arugula

200 g/7 oz. aged Gorgonzola
Piccante, crumbled

85 g/⅔ cup fresh coarsely
chopped walnuts

a handful of fresh flat-leaf parsley,
roughly chopped

4–6 tablespoons fruity extra virgin
olive oil

sea salt and freshly ground
black pepper

2 unwaxed lemons, halved, to serve

SERVES 4

This is my improvisation on the classic recipe and is very easy to prepare. Be sure to use prime ingredients, particularly when it comes to the beef.

Wrap the beef in clingfilm/plastic wrap and place in the freezer for 2 hours (this makes it easier to slice). Remove the plastic and, using a sharp filleting knife, cut the beef into paper-thin slices.

Cover four individual plates with the carpaccio slices. Rinse the rocket/arugula and place a mound on top. Sprinkle with the cheese, walnuts and parsley. Drizzle with the oil and season.

Serve with the lemon halves for squeezing over.

# Polpettone with courgette and lentil salad

**FOR THE POLPETTONE:**

250 g/9 oz. minced/ground beef

250 g/9 oz. minced/ground veal (preferably rose veal)

1 small red onion, very finely chopped

50 g/2 oz. thinly sliced pancetta, very finely chopped

1 garlic clove, crushed

grated zest of 1 unwaxed organic lemon

90 g/1½ cups fresh white breadcrumbs

3 tablespoons flat-leaf parsley

25 g/1¼ cup freshly grated Parmesan cheese

1 UK large/US extra-large egg, beaten

**FOR THE COURGETTE AND LENTIL SALAD:**

3 tablespoons garlic-infused extra virgin olive oil

375 g/scant 2 cups green lentils, rinsed

1 onion, halved

2 bay leaves

1 red (bell) pepper, deseeded and sliced

6 courgettes/zucchini, about 1 kg/2¼ lbs., cut into 5-mm/¼-in thick slices

freshly squeezed juice of 1 lemon

2 tablespoons extra virgin olive oil

2 tablespoons chopped fresh flat-leaf parsley

sea salt and freshly ground black pepper, to taste

**FOR THE SALSA VERDE:**

4 pickled cucumbers or big gherkins

a large bunch of fresh flat-leaf parsley

a large handful of fresh mint leaves

25 g/3 tablespoons salted capers, rinsed and dried

2 garlic cloves, peeled and chopped

2 large eggs, hard-boiled

4 tablespoons fresh white breadcrumbs

2 tablespoons white wine vinegar

1 tablespoon caster/granulated sugar

8 tablespoons extra virgin olive oil

a 1.5-litre/1½-quart loaf pan base-line with baking parchment

SERVES 4–6

Both the polpettone and the salad can be made in advance. The polpettone can be heated through or served cold and any leftovers make a delicious ciabatta filling. If you cannot find veal, use double the quantity of minced/ground beef.

Preheat the oven to 200°C (400°C) Gas 6.

Place the beef and veal in a mixing bowl and add the onion, pancetta, garlic, lemon zest, two-thirds of the breadcrumbs, parsley, Parmesan and egg. Season with a ¼ teaspoon salt and some pepper.

Tip the mixture into the prepared loaf pan and smooth out to the edges. Sprinkle the top with the remaining breadcrumbs. Cook in the preheated oven for 30 minutes until a skewer inserted into the centre of the meat feels piping hot to the touch. Take care not to burn your fingers! Leave to cool in the pan for at least 15 minutes, then lift out onto a plate.

For the salad, cook the lentils with 250 ml/1 cup water in a medium-sized pan with the onion and bay leaves. Add the (bell) pepper and courgettes/zucchini halfway through cooking. After 15 minutes, when the lentils are tender, add the lemon juice, oil and parsley, and season to taste.

Finally, for the salsa verde, finely chop the cucumbers or gherkins, parsley, mint, capers and garlic. Peel and mash the hard-boiled eggs. Put all the ingredients in a blender or food processor and blend everything together to produce a smooth, green sauce.

Serve slices of the polpettone on a bed of the lentil salad with the salsa verde spooned over the top.

# Salmoriglio lamb with borlotti and green bean salad

Salmoriglio is a Sicilian sauce of oregano and olive oil used for marinating fish and meat, or to dress salad. Here it is used to marinate lamb and doubles up as a salad dressing.

a 2-kg/4½-lb. butterflied leg of lamb

5 garlic cloves, 4 crushed, 1 whole

1 tablespoon chilli/hot red pepper flakes

3 tablespoons light brown sugar

thickly grated zest and freshly squeezed juice of 2 unwaxed, organic lemons

a small handful of oregano leaves, chopped

100 ml/6 tablespoons extra virgin olive oil

sea salt and freshly ground black pepper, to taste

**FOR THE BORLOTTI AND GREEN BEAN SALAD:**

3 red onions, cut into wedges

light brown sugar, to taste

3 tablespoons balsamic vinegar

2 x 400-g/14-oz. cans borlotti beans, drained and rinsed

300 g/11 oz. small vine-ripened tomatoes, halved

100 g/3½ oz. green beans, blanched

15 black olives, stoned/pitted

SERVES 6

Remove the lamb from the fridge and place in a large glass dish (or other non reactive container). Season.

For the marinade, mix the 4 crushed garlic cloves, the chilli/hot red pepper flakes, sugar, lemon zest, three-quarters of the lemon juice, half the oregano and 2 tablespoons of the olive oil in a small bowl. Pour the marinade over the lamb and massage it into the meat. Cover with clingfilm/plastic wrap and refrigerate for at least 2 hours. Remove the lamb from the fridge and bring it back to room temperature before cooking.

For the salad, preheat the oven to 180°C (350°F) Gas 4. Arrange the onions in a large roasting pan. Season well and drizzle with 2 tablespoons of the remaining olive oil, a little sugar and the balsamic vinegar. Roast in the preheated oven for 30 minutes. Put the borlotti beans in a serving dish and top them with the onions, tomatoes, green beans and olives. Finely chop the remaining oregano and garlic clove, top into a small bowl, add the remaining lemon juice and olive oil, whisk and season.

Heat a barbecue/gas or charcoal grill. Cook the lamb for 15 minutes on each side on indirect heat for pink meat. Leave to rest for 10 minutes. If cooking indoors, chargrill or sear the lamb in a hot griddle/grill pan or frying pan/skillet until browned on both sides, then finish in an oven preheated to 200°C (400°F) Gas 6 oven for 25–30 minutes.

Serve the meat sliced with the salad and the bowl of dressing.

# Oven-roasted rack of lamb with beetroot and walnut salsa

Get your butcher to French trim the racks so that they look neat and are easy to eat. Some supermarkets sell prepared French-trimmed racks of lamb.

10 beetroots/beets, about 1 kg/2¼ lbs., scrubbed clean

7 tablespoons extra virgin olive oil

4 garlic cloves, peeled but left whole

3–4 racks of lamb, about 1 kg/ 2¼ lbs. total weight

40 g/⅓ cup fresh walnut halves

1 tablespoon Dijon mustard

1½ tablespoons balsamic vinegar

1 tablespoon freshly squeezed lemon juice

2 tablespoons fresh mint leaves, finely chopped

50 g/2 large handfuls of rocket/ arugula

sea salt and freshly ground black pepper, to taste

SERVES 6

Preheat the oven to 200°C (400°F) Gas 6.

Place the beetroots/beets in a roasting pan and pour over 3 tablespoons of the olive oil. Mix well, add the garlic cloves and season with salt and pepper. Cover with foil and roast in the preheated oven for 1¼–1½ hours or until the beetroots/beets are cooked through but still firm.

Remove the beetroots/beets from the oven, leave until cool enough to handle, then peel off their skins and halve them. Return to the oven for a further 25 minutes. Remove from the oven but leave the oven on for the lamb. Discard the garlic cloves and leave the beetroots/beets to cool.

Place the racks of lamb in a large roasting pan and season well. Roast the lamb for 20–30 minutes, depending on how pink you like it, then remove from the oven, cover and leave to rest for 10 minutes.

Meanwhile, make the salsa. Heat a small frying pan/skillet and add the walnut halves. Dry-fry (without oil) over a moderate heat for 2–3 minutes, stirring, until lightly toasted. Remove from the heat, allow to cool, then roughly chop.

Finely dice the cooled beetroot flesh and place it in a mixing bowl. Add the remaining 4 tablespoons olive oil, the mustard, balsamic vinegar, lemon juice, cooled chopped walnuts and mint. Mix and season to taste. Roughly chop the rocket/arugula and stir it in.

To serve, either slice the lamb racks into individual chops, allowing three per person, or halve each rack. Serve with the salsa.

# Pork roast braised in milk with fresh herbs

Simmering a pork roast with milk and a generous handful of herbs results in very tender meat with rich silky juices. Many Italians will leave the milk curds that form alongside the meat where they are, but I strain them out for a more refined sauce.

50 ml/3 tablespoons olive oil

2–2.25-kg/4½–5-lb. boneless pork shoulder roast (without skin), tied

3 juniper berries, crushed

2 large sprigs of fresh rosemary

2 large sprigs of fresh sage

1 sprig of fresh or 4 dried bay leaves

1 garlic clove

1 teaspoon fine sea salt

½ teaspoon ground black pepper

50 ml/3 tablespoons white wine vinegar

1 litre/1 quart whole milk

extra sea salt and freshly ground black pepper, to taste

SERVES 6–8

Preheat the oven to 180°C (350°F) Gas 4 with the shelf/rack in the middle of the oven.

Heat the oil in a large, wide ovenproof heavy saucepan over a medium heat, then lightly brown the pork on all sides with the juniper berries and herbs for 8–10 minutes in total.

Add the garlic clove and sprinkle the pork with the fine sea salt and ground black pepper. Cook until the garlic is golden, about 1 minute. Pour the white wine vinegar over the roast and briskly simmer until it is reduced by half.

Pour the milk over the roast and bring to a bare simmer. Cover the saucepan and braise the pork in the oven, turning it occasionally, for 2–2½ hours until tender (the milk will form curds).

Transfer the roast to a carving board and loosely cover. Strain the juices through a fine-mesh sieve/strainer into a bowl (discard the solids) and skim off the fat. Return the juices to the saucepan and boil until flavourful and reduced to about 450 ml/2 cups. Season to taste with salt and pepper.

Slice the pork and serve it moistened with the juices.

# Sweet and sour spare ribs

This recipe has special memories for me. My mother made this when we were teenagers for family parties and gatherings. We were always eating Italian food, and when she produced this dish, we thought we were so exotic!

**2 kg/4½ lbs. pork spare ribs**

**sea salt**

**2 tablespoons groundnut/peanut oil**

**FOR THE SAUCE:**

**2 tablespoons groundnut/peanut oil**

**1 large white onion, finely chopped**

**1 large garlic clove, crushed**

**1 tablespoon cider vinegar**

**1 tablespoon tomato purée/paste**

**1 tablespoon tamari sauce**

**4 teaspoons soft light brown sugar**

**1 tablespoon clear honey**

**300 ml/1¼ cups good chicken stock (fresh is best)**

**freshly squeezed juice of 1 lemon**

**freshly ground black pepper**

SERVES 6–8

Preheat the oven to 190°C (375°F) Gas 5.

Sprinkle the pork with salt and place in a roasting pan. Pour over the oil and roast in the preheated oven for 25 minutes.

Meanwhile, prepare the sauce. Heat 1 tablespoon of the oil in a small saucepan, add the onion and fry/sauté gently until coloured. Add the garlic and gently cook until just softened. Add all the remaining sauce ingredients to the pan, along with ground pepper to taste and mix well.

Remove the pork from the oven, transfer to a chopping board and use a sharp knife to cut it into individual ribs. Return the ribs to the roasting pan, pour over the sauce and continue to roast, covered with foil, for a further 1–1½ hours.

Serve with cooked white rice or your own favourite accompaniment.

# Sweet, sticky Chinese chicken

4 Maryland pieces of chicken
(leg and thigh together)

**FOR THE MARINADE:**

grated zest and juice of 1 unwaxed
organic orange

3 tablespoons clear honey

2 tablespoons muscovado/
light brown sugar

1 tablespoon Chinese five-spice
powder

2 tablespoons soy sauce

2 tablespoons toasted sesame oil

**TO SERVE:**

crisp green salad

SERVES 8

As an Italian, I love Italian food. However, as I live with a gourmet husband whose palate extends across the globe, I sometimes have to step outside Italy. This easy, home-from-work recipe fits the bill.

Put the chicken in a sealable plastic bag. Mix all the marinade ingredients together and pour over the chicken. Seal the bag and squidge it together to coat the chicken well. Refrigerate for at least 2 hours (overnight is better).

Preheat the oven to 180°C (350°F) Gas 4. Tip the chicken and marinade into a large roasting pan and spread it out evenly. Roast in the preheated oven for 45 minutes until the chicken is cooked through with no pink meat, and the juices run clear.

Remove the cooked chicken from the oven and, if liked, finish in a hot griddle/grill pan, browning the pieces skin-side down for about 5 minutes until the chicken is crisp and slightly charred. Serve with a crisp green salad.

# Nonna Ferrigno's chicken casserole

2 tablespoons Italian 'oo' flour, seasoned with fine sea salt and ground black pepper

8 chicken thighs, bone and skin on or off, depending on preference

3 tablespoons olive oil

2 celery stalks/ribs, finely chopped

1 medium carrot, diced

1 red onion, diced

150 g/5½ oz. chestnut/cremini mushrooms, coarsely chopped

1 garlic clove, crushed

3 tablespoons white wine vinegar

2 sprigs of fresh rosemary, leaves finely chopped

1 teaspoon dried mixed herbs

3 fresh or 2 dried bay leaves

6 tablespoons Italian passata/sieved tomatoes

6 medium potatoes, peeled and quartered

a handful of fresh flat-leaf parsley leaves, chopped

sea salt and freshly ground black pepper, to taste

TO SERVE:

focaccia or crusty bread

SERVES 8

This recipe is revisited so frequently in my home, not just for its taste, but also for its ease of cooking. It is tasty, satisfying and also a one-pot meal, which is very useful for the time-short. I have experimented over the years with various combinations, sometimes using smoky bacon, lardons or pancetta. All of these are good additions.

Put the flour on a plate. Add the chicken thighs and toss to coat them.

Set a flameproof casserole dish over the hob/stovetop. Add the olive oil and heat gently. Add the flour-dusted chicken, cook until coloured all over and then remove. Add more oil if necessary then add the celery, carrot, onion, mushrooms and garlic to the dish. Cook for 5 minutes until lightly golden. Return the chicken to the dish, add the vinegar, 500 ml/2 cups cold water, herbs, passata/sieved tomatoes and potatoes. Season well with salt and pepper.

Simmer gently, covered, for 45 minutes, checking that the casserole is not drying up and stirring it periodically to avoid it catching on the bottle of the dish.

Garnish with the parsley and serve spooned into soup plates with focaccia or crusty bread to mop up the juices.

# Marinated duck breasts
# with cucumber and mint salad

This recipe is a little bit more demanding in terms of ingredients and effort, but it is well worth it! The combination of Asian flavours is very authentic, making the dish a perennial hit with my family and dinner guests alike.

**FOR THE MARINADE:**

1 cinnamon stick

1 star anise

2 teaspoons coriander seeds

a 3-cm/1¼-in. piece of fresh ginger, peeled and grated

2 medium shallots, finely diced

1 tablespoon sea salt

3 tablespoons rice vinegar

2 duck breasts

**FOR THE CUCUMBER AND MINT SALAD:**

125 g/4½ oz. cucumber, sliced in matchsticks

1 teaspoon sea salt

1 red onion, finely chopped

2 tablespoons white wine vinegar

1 tablespoon rapeseed/canola oil

2 tablespoons fruity extra virgin olive oil

1 tablespoon caster/granulated sugar

a large handful of fresh mint leaves, chopped

a bag of pea shoots, approximately 110 g/4 oz.

SERVES 4

To make the marinade, dry fry the spices (without oil) in a frying pan/skillet for 1½–2 minutes until fragrant. Transfer to a mortar and add the ginger and shallots. Pound with a pestle until soft then mix in the salt and rice vinegar. Use your hands to rub this paste over the duck breasts and put them in a glass dish. Cover with clingfilm/plastic wrap and refrigerate for a minimum of 2 hours or ideally overnight.

For the salad, toss the cucumber with 1 teaspoon salt in a colander. Drain in the sink for 20 minutes. Scatter the cucumber slices on paper towels and pat dry. Soak the red onion in iced water for 10 minutes, then drain.

Mix the cucumber, red onion, vinegar, oils, sugar and mint together in a bowl. Season with salt and pepper, and set aside.

Preheat the oven to 180°C (350°C) Gas 4.

Brush the marinade off the duck breasts and place them skin-side down in a cold, ovenproof frying pan/skillet. Cook over a medium heat for 15 minutes, and pour away any excess fat. Turn the breasts over and cook for 2 minutes, then place the frying pan/skillet in the preheated oven for 10 minutes.

Add the pea shoots ot the cucumber salad and stir in. Slice the duck breast and toss through the salad. Spoon onto plates and serve.

# VEGETARIAN DISHES

## Potato gnocchi with truffle oil and sage

Gnocchi should be feather-light and airy, and the use of a floury potato is essential for great results. The varieties that I recommend are Rooster, King Edward, Pentland Crown and American Russet. Baking the potatoes achieves great results. I think it is slightly easier too, plus you get a really great flavour from the baked potato, which has a distinctive nutty taste close to the skin.

**750 g/1 lb. 10 oz. even-sized floury old potatoes**

**150 g/1 cup plus 3 tablespoons Italian 'oo' flour**

**1 teaspoon fine sea salt**

**1 teaspoon white/black truffle paste, optional**

**1 UK large/US extra large egg, lightly beaten**

**75 g/5 tablespoons unsalted butter**

**a handful of large fresh sage leaves**

**1 tablespoon truffle-infused olive oil**

**fresh truffle shavings, optional**

**TO SERVE:**

**75 g/¾ cup freshly grated Parmesan cheese**

SERVES 4–6

Preheat the oven to 200°C (400°F) Gas 6.

Place the potatoes on a baking sheet lined with baking parchment and bake for 40–45 minutes. If the potatoes are tender, they are cooked.

Leave to cool slightly. Cut the potatoes in half and scoop out the flesh. Place the flesh in a ricer or Mouli grater and process directly onto the work surface. Scatter the flour around the riced potatoes, make a well in the centre and add the salt, truffle paste (if using) and the egg. Mix gently until you have a soft dough. Add more flour as needed, taking care not to overwork the dough. Shape it into long, narrow logs. Wrap each log in clingfilm/plastic wrap and leave to rest for 10 minutes.

Slowly melt the butter in a medium saucepan set over a low heat. Add the sage leaves.

Roll the rested dough into a narrow sausage, 1 cm/½ in. thick. Cut the log into short 2-cm/¾-in. pieces and pinch the gnocchi to create texture for the sauce. You may like to roll the gnocchi over the back of the tines of a fork. Set aside on a floured tray and keep covered.

Bring a large saucepan of salted water to a rolling boil and drop in the gnocchi in batches. When the gnocchi rise to the surface, count to 30, remove the gnocchi and add them to the warm butter. Add the truffle oil, truffle shavings, if using, and Parmesan cheese, then serve.

# Sweet and sour peppers with mozzarella

6 (bell) peppers, a mixture of red, yellow and orange

3 tablespoons white wine vinegar

6 tablespoons fruity extra virgin olive oil, Ligurian if possible

50 g/⅓ cup sultanas/golden raisins

1½ teaspoons cumin seeds

1 teaspoon crushed dried peperoncini chillies/chiles

1 garlic clove, finely sliced

2 teaspoons caster/granulated sugar

sea salt and freshly ground black pepper, to taste

**FOR THE SALAD:**

3 x 125-g/4½-oz. balls fresh buffalo mozzarella, sliced

6 Queen Spanish or other large green olives, stoned/pitted and sliced lengthways

60 g/2¼ oz. rocket/arugula

1 tablespoon extra virgin olive oil, light and not too bold in flavour

**TO SERVE:**

crusty bread for mopping up juices

SERVES 4–6

This antipasto is timeless and its colour, simplicity and flavour always hit the right key. It is ideal for those with busy lives, as it can be made days in advance. There was always some roasted pepper in my Nonna's kitchen to dip crusty bread into as a wonderful snack.

Preheat the oven to 200°C (400°F) Gas 6.

Place the peppers on a baking sheet lined with baking parchment and bake for 25 minutes until slightly blackened and deflated. Leave to cool. Peel the peppers and discard the seeds, then cut into 1-cm/½-in. strips.

Mix the pepper strips with the vinegar, oil, sultanas/golden raisins, cumin and peperoncini chillies/chiles. Season to taste. Add the garlic and sugar and leave to infuse.

To serve, divide the mozzarella between 4–6 plates, spoon over the pepper mixture and scatter over the olives. Toss the rocket/arugula leaves in the oil and scatter some on each plate. Serve immediately.

# Panisse with aubergine & pine nut caviar

**FOR THE PANCAKES:**

250 g/2 cups chickpea/gram flour, sifted

½ teaspoon ground cumin

1 teaspoon fine sea salt

6 tablespoons olive oil

2–3 tablespoons groundnut/peanut oil

**FOR THE CAVIAR:**

3 medium-sized aubergines/eggplant

6 tablespoons fruity extra virgin olive oil, with citrus notes

1 red onion, finely chopped

sea salt and freshly ground black pepper

100 g/⅔ cup pine nuts, toasted in a dry frying pan/skillet

6 sprigs of fresh mint leaves, plus extra, chopped, to serve

a small handful of fresh flat-leaf parsley

a small handful of fresh coriander/cilantro

freshly squeezed juice of 1 lemon

3 tablespoons light tahini paste

1 garlic clove

paprika to taste, and for garnishing

2 small pinches of chilli/chili powder

**TO SERVE:**

300 g/1¼ cups plain yogurt

a frying pan/skillet about 18 cm/7 in. in diameter

SERVES 4–6

A delicious Provençal snack, these gluten-free pancakes make a delicious treat.

For the pancake batter, put the flour, cumin and salt in a mixing bowl. Make a well in the centre and pour in the olive oil. Gradually whisk in 450 ml/2 cups of water to make a smooth batter. Leave to rest in a cool place for at least 2 hours.

For the caviar, preheat the oven to 200°C (400°F) Gas 6. Put two of the aubergines/eggplants on a lined baking sheet. Bake in the preheated oven for 45 minutes until soft and shrivelled. Meanwhile, dice the remaining aubergine/eggplant into 1-cm/½-in. pieces. Heat 3 tablespoons of the olive oil in a saucepan and add the onion and a pinch of salt. Cook, stirring over a moderate heat, for 10 minutes until the onion is soft. Add the diced aubergine/eggplant and continue to cook, stirring, for 15–20 minutes until tender. Season to taste. Stir two-thirds of the toasted pine nuts into the onion and aubergine/eggplant mixture and reserve the rest for garnish.

When the aubergines/eggplant in the oven are cooked, remove and leave to cool. Split in half and scoop out the flesh into a sieve/strainer over a bowl. Press down to remove excess water. Place the flesh in a blender or food processor and add the mint, parsley, coriander/cilantro, lemon juice, tahini paste, garlic clove, paprika and chilli/chili powder. Blend until smooth and add the remaining 3 tablespoons olive oil. Season to taste. Mix the purée with the onion, aubergine/eggplant and pine nut mixture and keep it warm while you prepare the pancakes.

Heat the groundnut/peanut oil in the frying pan/skillet. Add a ladleful of batter and cook for about 2 minutes, then carefully flip and cook for 1 minute. Slide the pancake onto a lined baking sheet. Cook the rest of the batter this way, adding more oil to the pan if necessary.

To serve, place a pancake on a plate and top with the caviar and a little yogurt. Scatter with chopped mint and the remaining pine nuts.

# Spaghetti with oven-roasted tomatoes, thyme and peppered Pecorino

This is a simple but flavoursome recipe that can be prepared in several ways. The common denominator is fresh lemon thyme, which helps blend the tomatoes with the peppery, spicy taste of the Pecorino. In the winter use oven-roasted tomatoes because they are more savoury, but during the summer months try using fresh ones if you can.

400 g/14 oz. ripe cherry tomatoes on the vine (smell the stalk end for a peppery scent)

4 teaspoons fresh lemon thyme, finely chopped

2 garlic cloves, finely chopped

6 tablespoons grapeseed oil

a handful of fresh basil leaves, torn

400 g/14 oz. dried spaghetti

90 g/3¼ oz. peppered/regular Pecorino shavings

3 tablespoons estate-bottled extra virgin olive oil

sea salt and freshly ground black pepper, to taste

SERVES 4

Preheat the oven to 150°C (300°F) Gas 2.

Place the tomatoes on a baking sheet, cut-sides up. Sprinkle with the thyme, garlic and half of the oil, and roast in the preheated oven for 1 hour. Leave to cool.

Heat the remaining oil in a large, deep-sided frying pan/skillet over a low heat and add the tomatoes and basil. Season with salt and pepper.

Cook the pasta in a large saucepan of boiling salted water until al dente. Drain well.

Transfer the pasta to the tomatoes in the pan. Add the Pecorino shavings and extra virgin olive oil, toss and serve immediately with a peppery green salad.

# Orecchiette with chickpeas

You can barely take a step in Puglia without encountering homemade orecchiette (Italian for 'little ear'). They are made from semolina and contain no eggs (unlike pasta) and are an ideal shape to pair with tender chickpeas.

**FOR THE SAUCE:**

**100 g/½ cup plus 2 tablespoons dried chickpeas, soaked overnight**

**2 garlic cloves, left whole, plus 4 garlic cloves, finely chopped**

**3 bay leaves**

**150 ml/⅔ cup olive oil**

**1 medium onion, finely chopped**

**2 celery stalks/ribs, finely chopped**

**2 medium carrots, finely chopped**

**¼–½ teaspoon crushed, dried peperoncini chillies/chiles**

**1 teaspoon fine sea salt**

**350 g/12 oz. vine-ripened tomatoes, finely chopped**

**a handful of fresh flat-leaf parsley leaves, finely chopped**

**FOR THE ORECCHIETTE:**

**¾ teaspoon fine sea salt**

**225 g/1¾ cups semolina, plus extra for sprinkling**

**grated Pecorino or Parmesan cheese, to serve**

2 trays lined with kitchen towels and dusted with semolina

SERVES 8

Drain the chickpeas and transfer to a large saucepan. Add fresh water to cover by 5 cm/2 in., plus the whole garlic cloves and bay leaves. Partially cover the pan with a lid and simmer for 1–1¼ hours, until the chickpeas are tender, adding more water if necessary. Drain, reserve the chickpeas and discard the garlic and bay leaves.

Heat the olive oil in a large, heavy-based saucepan set over a medium heat. Cook the onion, celery, carrots, chopped garlic, peperoncini and ½ teaspoon of the salt (covered but stirring occasionally) for about 12 minutes, until the vegetables are soft. Add the cooked chickpeas, tomatoes, 225 ml/1 scant cup water and the remaining ½ teaspoon salt and simmer, uncovered, for about 5 minutes, until the vegetables are tender and the sauce has slightly thickened. Stir in the parsley and season to taste.

For the orecchiette, stir together 110 ml/½ scant cup warm water (40–45°C/105–115°F) and the salt in a bowl until the salt has dissolved. Add the semolina in a stream, beating with an electric mixer at medium speed for about 2 minutes, until a stiff dough forms. Transfer the dough to a work surface lightly dusted with semolina and knead with lightly dusted hands until smooth and elastic, about 6 minutes. Divide the dough into 5 pieces of equal size and let these stand under an overturned bowl for 30 minutes.

Take one piece of the dough (keeping the remaining dough covered to stop it drying out) and roll it into a 35-cm/14-in-long rope (about 2 cm/¾ in. thick) on an unfloured surface. Cut this rope into ½-cm/¼-in. pieces. Dust your thumb with some semolina and press down on each piece of dough, pushing away from you and twisting your thumb slightly to form an indented curled shape (like an ear). Transfer to the prepared trays. Repeat with the rest of the dough.

Bring a pan of salted water to a rolling boil, add the orecchiette and cook until they are al dente. Drain and toss with the sauce.

## FOR THE SEVEN-VEGETABLE TAGINE:

125 g/¾ cup dried chickpeas, soaked overnight

2 large white onions, finely chopped

2 garlic cloves, finely chopped

½ teaspoon saffron threads

2 teaspoons ground cinnamon

1 teaspoon paprika

a large pinch of cayenne pepper

½ teaspoon ground ginger

1 tablespoon ras el hanout spice mix

a pinch of fine sea salt

225 g/8 oz. carrots, halved lengthways

½ medium white cabbage, cut into 8 pieces

6 artichoke hearts

1 aubergine/eggplant, quartered

225 g/8 oz. new potatoes, peeled and halved

225 g/8 oz. turnips, peeled and sliced

225 g/8 oz. broad/fava beans, skinned

125 g/1 scant cup raisins

225 g/8 oz. fresh pumpkin, cut into 5-cm/2-in. slices

2 tomatoes

a bunch of fresh flat-leaf parsley, chopped

a large bunch of fresh coriander/cilantro, chopped

1 tablespoon olive oil

## FOR THE COUSCOUS:

450 g/2⅔ cups quick-cook couscous

a pinch of fine sea salt

4 tablespoons French extra virgin olive oil

1–2 tablespoons unsalted butter

SERVES 5–6

# Seven-vegetable tagine with steamed couscous

Couscous is the national dish of Morocco. In Morocco it is more delicate and less hot and spicy than the Tunisian and Algerian versions now found in France. Seven, considered a lucky number, is the traditional number of vegetables used in the recipe, the choice depending on those in season. This is a one-pot meal, easy to make for large numbers.

Drain the chickpeas and transfer to a large stockpot. Add 3 litres/quarts of fresh water. Bring to the boil and skim off the froth. Add the onions and garlic along with all the spices. Partially cover the pan with a lid and simmer for at least 30 minutes, adding more water if necessary. Season with a pinch of salt when the chickpeas begin to soften.

Add the carrots, cabbage, artichoke hearts, aubergine/eggplant and potatoes, and more water, if necessary and cook for 20 minutes. Add the turnips, broad/fava beans and raisins and cook for 10 minutes. Next, add the pumpkin and tomatoes and cook for 5 minutes. Finally add the herbs and oil and cook for a further 5 minutes.

While the vegetables are cooking, prepare the couscous. Put the couscous in a large bowl and pour in 300 ml/1¼ cups cold water with the salt. Stir well until evenly absorbed. Leave for 10 minutes. Add a further 300 ml/1¼ cups of water along with the oil and butter. Rub the grains between your palms and make sure that they are all separate. Leave for a further 10 minutes until the grains are swollen and tender but separate. Tip the couscous into a fine mesh metal sieve/strainer and set it over a vegetable steamer. Steam the couscous, uncovered, over boiling water for about 8 minutes. (When the steam begins to come through the grain, it is ready to serve.)

Turn the couscous onto a large warmed serving dish and crush with a fork to separate the grains. Put the vegetables in the centre and serve immediately.

# Radicchio lasagne

I have a tremendous love of radicchio, having watched it being grown by my father. It's great to grow at home, as it is ready to harvest in just six weeks. There are two varieties: round radicchio, which is the most common, and Treviso, which is long and thin. Do try and get Treviso – order it from your greengrocer if needs be – as it is much less bitter and much more flavourful.

**4 heads Treviso radicchio or 2 medium round radicchio**

**4 tablespoons/¼ cup olive oil**

**1 medium fennel bulb, stalks and outer layer discarded, and quartered**

**300 g/11 oz. dried lasagne verdi (green pasta sheets)**

**85 g/6 tablespoons unsalted butter**

**1 red onion, finely chopped**

**55 g/½ cup plain/all-purpose flour**

**1 garlic clove, crushed**

**500 ml/2 cups whole milk**

**150 g/5½ oz. Gorgonzola cheese, cut into cubes**

**sea salt and freshly ground black pepper, to taste**

a deep-sided ovenproof baking dish, lightly oiled

SERVES 4

Preheat the oven to 200°C (400°F) Gas 6.

Quarter the radicchio, wash well and pat dry. Place on a baking sheet and drizzle the radicchio with the oil. Bake in the preheated oven (or put under a preheated grill/broiler) for 10 minutes. The radicchio will change colour and become slightly charred. This is correct, as the flavour will be at its best. Set aside. Leave the oven on to cook the finished dish.

Meanwhile, steam the fennel pieces over boiling water, about 12 minutes (it should be slightly al dente). Remove and finely chop.

Cook the lasagne sheets in plenty of rolling boiling, salted water until al dente. Drain and set aside.

Heat the butter in a saucepan set over a low-to-medium heat, add the onion and cook until it is softened and golden. Add the flour, garlic and steamed fennel and cook for a few minutes to remove the raw taste from the flour. Now add the milk, and season to taste. Remove from the heat and stir vigorously with a wooden spoon.

Put the pan back on the heat and bring to the boil, stirring continuously until thickened. Add the cubed Gorgonzola and stir well. Season to taste.

To assemble the dish, place a layer of sauce in the prepared ovenproof dish, followed by a layer of radicchio and a layer of pasta, and continue in this fashion until all the sauce, radicchio and lasagne sheets have been used up. Finish with sauce on top.

Place in the preheated oven and bake for 20 minutes until golden. Serve hot with a green salad.

# Roman artichokes

Artichokes grow all over Italy, but the Lazio region, and Rome in particular, is especially renowned for its small, tender artichokes. Speciality dishes feature on restaurant menus throughout the capital during artichoke season. Try to buy young artichokes with long stalks, as these are tender and won't yet have developed much in the way of a choke. For this appetizer, the artichokes are best served warm.

**4 medium globe artichokes**

**1 unwaxed organic lemon, halved**

**3 fresh bay leaves**

**150 ml/⅔ cup dry white wine**

**FOR THE DRESSING:**

**a large handful of fresh mint leaves, finely chopped**

**2 garlic cloves, finely chopped**

**3–4 tablespoons extra virgin olive oil**

**2 tablespoons white wine vinegar**

**sea salt and freshly ground black pepper, to taste**

SERVES 4

Prepare the artichokes one at a time. Trim the base of the stalk at an angle, then peel the stem. Cut off the leaves about ½ cm/¼ in. from the top. Rub the cut surfaces with a lemon half. Now start peeling away the artichoke leaves, removing at least four layers, until the leaves begin to look pale. Spread the top leaves and use a teaspoon to scrape out the choke. Immerse the artichoke in a bowl of cold water with the other lemon half added (to prevent discolouration). Repeat to prepare the rest of the artichokes.

Place the bay leaves, lemon halves, wine and artichokes in a large saucepan and add enough cold water to cover (the artichokes should fit snugly in the pan). Bring to the boil, cover and simmer for about 30–35 minutes until the artichokes are tender. Drain the artichokes thoroughly.

To make the dressing, place the chopped mint leaves and garlic in a bowl with the oil and vinegar. Season to taste and whisk thoroughly to blend.

Arrange the artichokes upside down (with their stalks sticking up) on serving plates. Pour the dressing over the warm artichokes and serve.

# Tian of baked courgettes

Some Provençal dishes take their name from the local earthenware casserole, the tian, in which they are cooked. This particular recipe, provided by Martine Bourdon-Williams of Nice, has a pleasant mixture of different textures and flavours as it features chewy rice as well as spinach, green herbs and Parmesan cheese.

**1.5 kg/3¼ lbs. tender young courgettes/zucchini**

**225 g/8 oz. short-grain rice**

**3 tablespoons olive oil**

**2 large onions, finely chopped**

**1 garlic clove, finely chopped**

**3 UK medium/US large eggs**

**225 g/8 oz. young spinach leaves, shredded**

**a large handful of fresh flat-leaf parsley, finely chopped**

**a handful fresh basil leaves, torn**

**100 g/1 cup freshly grated Parmesan cheese**

**2 tablespoons French extra virgin olive oil**

**sea salt and freshly ground black pepper, to taste**

**a large ovenproof dish, greased with olive oil**

SERVES 8

Trim the courgettes/zucchini but leave them whole and unpeeled. Boil in a saucepan of salted water for 10 minutes, or steam until tender.

Cook the rice in a separate saucepan of boiling, salted water for 10 minutes, then drain.

Heat 2 tablespoons of the olive oil in a frying pan/skillet. Add the onion and garlic and sauté for 5 minutes until golden.

Preheat the oven to 200°C (400°F) Gas 6.

Turn the cooked courgettes/zucchini into a colander and mash with a potato masher, letting the juices drain away.

In a large bowl, lightly beat the eggs and add the spinach, parsley, basil, Parmesan and pepper, then add the mashed courgettes/zucchini, garlic and onion, along with the rice. Mix well together and taste before adding any salt.

Pour the mixture into the prepared dish and bake in the oven for 30 minutes or until firm and browned on top. Drizzle with the extra virgin olive oil and serve.

# Leek and chickpeas with mustard dressing

**5 tablespoons rapeseed/canola oil**

**4 medium leeks, washed well and finely chopped**

**fine sea salt**

**400 g/2 cups cooked chickpeas (⅓ crushed to absorb more flavour)**

**a handful of fresh flat-leaf parsley, finely chopped**

**3 tablespoons freshly ground black pepper**

**1 tablespoon Dijon mustard**

**1 teaspoon wholegrain mustard**

**1 tablespoon white wine vinegar**

SERVES 4–6

This is a relaxed dish to serve with meat or fish, or as an appetizer with sourdough on the side. It improves in flavour over time, so it's a good idea to make it in advance.

Heat 2 tablespoons of the rapeseed/canola oil in a frying pan/skillet, add the leeks and salt to taste and cook until softened. Add the chickpeas, mix well and heat well together. Take off the heat and add the parsley and black pepper.

Mix the mustards, vinegar and remaining oil together, then stir into the leeks and chickpeas and serve.

# Italian-style green vegetables

200 g/7 oz. trimmed green beans

200 g/7 oz. tenderstem broccoli

100 g/3½ oz. young spinach leaves

grated zest and freshly squeezed juice of 1 unwaxed organic lemon

1 mild fresh red chilli/chile, deseeded and finely chopped or a pinch of crushed dried peperoncini chillies/chiles

100 ml/6 tablespoons fruity extra virgin olive oil – Sicilian if possible

sea salt and freshly ground black pepper, to taste

SERVES 4–6

This very simple treatment of green vegetables is enduringly delicious, Antonia, my little girl, will not eat vegetables done any other way with quite the same relish!

Bring a large pan of water to the boil. Plunge all the vegetables in it for 3 minutes. Drain immediately and place in a bowl.

Add the lemon zest and juice and combine with the extra virgin olive oil. Add the chilli/chile and season the dressing to taste.

Stir the dressing through the vegetables to coat.

# BREADS

## Potato and gorgonzola focaccia

**FOR THE DOUGH:**

2 medium potatoes, peeled and chopped

500–550g/4–4⅓ cups white strong/bread flour, plus extra for sprinkling and kneading

2 teaspoons fine sea salt

15 g/½ oz. fresh yeast, crumbled or 7 g/¼ oz. dried/active dry yeast

250 ml/1 cup water at body temperature

3 tablespoons olive oil

**FOR THE TOPPING:**

1 x 400-g/14-oz. can Italian plum tomatoes, drained and chopped

1 tablespoon fresh oregano, chopped

2 tablespoons fresh basil, torn

1 garlic glove, finely chopped

½ teaspoon freshly ground black pepper

375 g/13 oz. quartered artichoke hearts in marinated olive oil

250 g/9 oz. Gorgonzola cheese, crumbled

150 g/5½ oz. mozzarella, shredded

**TO SERVE:**

fruity extra virgin olive oil

a 38 x 25 x 2.5 cm/15 x 10 x 1 in. baking sheet, greased

MAKES 1

Potato in dough is quite remarkable. This is a firm family favourite for sharing at gatherings or picnics.

Put the potatoes in a saucepan with plenty of water and bring to the boil. Cook, covered, for 10–15 minutes until tender. Drain and return to the pan. Mash and leave to cool slightly.

In a large bowl, mix two thirds of the flour with the salt. Dissolve the yeast in 2 tablespoons of the water and add it to a well in the centre of the flour with the olive oil. Mix for a few minutes, then stir in the mashed potatoes and as much of the remaining flour as you can.

On a lightly floured work surface, knead in enough of the remaining flour to make a stiff dough that is both smooth and elastic. This will take about 8–10 minutes. Shape the dough into a ball and place it in an oiled bowl, turning it once to grease the surface. Cover it with a damp, clean dish towel and leave it to rise for about 1 hour in a warm place until it has doubled in size.

Knock back the dough, cover and let it rest for 10 minutes. Press the dough into the prepared baking sheet. If it is sticky, sprinkle the surface with about 1 tablespoon of extra flour. Using your fingertips, make small indentations in the dough. Cover and leave it to prove for about 30 minutes, until it has nearly doubled in size.

Meanwhile, preheat the oven to 190°C (375°F) Gas 5.

For the topping, mix the tomatoes, oregano, basil, garlic and pepper and spoon evenly over the dough. Place the artichoke hearts over the tomato sauce mixture. Cover with the Gorgonzola and shredded mozzarella. Bake in the preheated oven for 35 minutes. Serve hot, drizzled with the extra virgin olive oil.

# Sardinian pizza

I have always dreamed of opening a pizzeria, and I think that this particular recipe would be my signature pizza.

**FOR THE PIZZA DOUGH:**

15 g/½ oz. fresh yeast or
7 g/¼ oz. dried/active dry yeast

4 tablespoons water at body temperature

225 g/1¾ cups white strong/bread flour, plus extra for sprinkling

1 teaspoon fine sea salt

65 g/2¼ oz. unsalted butter

1 UK large/US extra large egg, beaten

olive oil

**FOR THE TOPPING:**

5 tablespoons olive oil

750 g/1 lb. 10 oz. onions, finely sliced

500g/1 lb. 2 oz. ripe tomatoes, skinned and roughly chopped

sea salt and freshly ground black pepper, to taste

55 g/2 oz. anchovy fillets

a handful of black olives, halved and stoned/pitted

a handful of fresh oregano

**TO SERVE:**

chilli/chili oil

SERVES 8

To make the pizza dough, blend the yeast with the water. Mix the flour and salt together in a large bowl, rub in the butter and make a well in the centre. Put in the egg and the yeast mixture and combine to a firm but pliable dough, adding more water if necessary. When the dough has come away cleanly from the sides of the bowl, turn out onto a floured work surface and knead thoroughly for 10 minutes. Gather into a ball, place into a clean oiled bowl and cover and leave to rise until doubled in size, about 1½ hours.

When the dough has risen, turn it out onto a floured work surface, divide into two and knead each piece lightly. Place in two well-oiled 20–23 cm/8–9 in. pans and press out with floured knuckles. Cover the pans and preheat the oven to 200°C (400°F) Gas 6, while you prepare the topping.

To make the topping, heat 5 tablespoons of the olive oil in a heavy-bottomed frying pan/skillet and sauté the onion gently, covered, stirring now and then, until soft, about 20 minutes. Add the tomatoes and seasoning and cook, uncovered, until the sauce is thick. Leave to cool.

When cold, divide the topping between the pizzas, spreading it evenly. Criss-cross the surface with strips of anchovy and put the olive halves in the spaces. Sprinkle with oregano and bake in the preheated oven for 25 minutes, until golden brown and bubbling. Drizzle with chilli/chili oil before serving.

# Herbed wholegrain spelt bread

This bread has become a real passion of mine and I serve it to guests whenever I possibly can. If I was a betting woman, I would put money on this flour becoming more and more important in the future. It does contain gluten, but it is wheat-free, and as a teacher, I am finding that more and more of my students suffer from food intolerances. As this bread is a one-rise bread, it is easy to fit around our hectic lifestyles. Because of the short protein strands of the grain, a short knead and one rise is all that is necessary. Please feel free to experiment with white and wholegrain. I love the nutty texture of this bread and I sometimes even make grissini with this dough.

500 g/4 cups wholegrain spelt flour, plus extra for sprinkling and kneading

2 teaspoons fine sea salt

3 teaspoons fresh rosemary needles, coarsely chopped

2 teaspoons freshly ground black pepper

2 tablespoons rapeseed/canola oil

1 tablespoon fragrant honey such as acacia or rosemary honey

7 g/¼ oz. fresh yeast or 1 teaspoon dried/active dry yeast

400 ml/1¾ cups water at body temperature

a baking sheet lined with parchment

MAKES 2

In a large bowl, add the flour, salt, rosemary and black pepper and mix well. Make a reservoir in the middle of the flour, add the oil and honey and then the yeast and water.

Mix well and turn the mixture out of the bowl onto a lightly floured work surface. Knead for about 8 minutes, adding more flour as necessary, until the dough is strong, soft and silky.

Shape into two baguettes and place side by side on the prepared baking sheet. Cover with a clean kitchen cloth and leave for 40 minutes.

Preheat the oven to 180°C (360°F) Gas 5.

Bake the loaves in the preheated oven until they are golden brown and sound hollow when you tap the underside. Cool on a wire rack.

Dip in olive oil or spread with butter to serve.

# Olive oil and black pepper biscuits

These crunchy little savoury biscuits called 'tarelli' hail from Puglia and are very addictive. We serve these in Italy with aperitivos, but they are also excellent picnic snacks. In Puglia these are available everywhere, but homemade ones are unparalleled. Try adding fennel seeds as they work very well too.

**150 g /1 cup plus 3 tablespoons Italian 'oo' flour, plus extra for sprinkling and kneading**

**40 g/⅓ cup semolina (fine)**

**1 teaspoon freshly ground black pepper or 2 teaspoons lightly crushed fennel seeds (if using)**

**2 teaspoons fine sea salt**

**70 ml/⅓ cup dry white wine**

**70 ml/⅓ cup extra virgin olive oil, an Italian one from Puglia if possible**

**2 oiled baking sheets**

MAKES 30

Put the flour, semolina, pepper (or fennel seeds, if preferred) and half the salt in a large bowl. Add the wine and oil and mix to combine. Turn out onto a floured surface and knead for about 2 minutes, until the dough is smooth and elastic. Place the dough in a lightly oiled bowl, cover with a clean kitchen towel and leave to relax for about 45 minutes to 1 hour.

Halve the relaxed dough and cut each half into 10 pieces. Keep the remaining dough covered as you work to stop it drying out. Roll one piece of dough into a 50-cm/10-in. long rope. Cut the rope into 5 pieces, then roll each piece into 10-cm/4-in. ropes. Connect the ends to form an overlapping ring. Continue with the remaining dough, keeping the rings covered too, as you make them.

Preheat the oven to 180°C (350°F) Gas 5. Bring 900 ml/scant 4 cups water to the boil in a large saucepan and add the remaining salt.

Add the rings to the saucepan of boiling water in batches and cook for about 3 minutes, until they float. Use a slotted spoon to transfer them to the prepared baking sheets. Bake in the preheated oven for about 30 minutes, until golden and crisp, Let cool on wire racks before serving with drinks as a nibble.

# PRESERVES, MARINADES & DRESSINGS

## Dried tomatoes stuffed with anchovies and capers

**2 kg/4½ lbs. good plum tomatoes (smell the stalk end for a peppery scent)**

**75 g/⅓ cup salted capers, rinsed at least twice and finely chopped**

**75 g/2¾ oz. anchovy fillets, finely chopped**

**4 dried chillies/chiles (peperoncini), or more to taste**

**6 garlic cloves, blanched briefly in boiling water and finely chopped**

**extra virgin olive oil (from Puglia if possible) to fill the jars**

MAKES 6 X 350-G/12-OZ. JARS

Tomatoes can become a problem in Italy, but only because we have so many that all seem to ripen at the same time! The best tomato for southern Italians is undisputedly the San Marzano tomato – the tomato with attitude. It has a great flavour for sauces and also this preserve, which brings back a rush of childhood memories, possibly stronger than any other dish in the book.

Preheat the oven to 140°C (275°F) Gas 1.

Pour water into a pan large enough to hold all the tomatoes at the same time, and bring to the boil. Add the tomatoes when the water is boiling. Just a couple of minutes is enough to soften the skins slightly.

Drain the tomatoes, then cut them in half and spread out on a baking sheet. Place in the preheated oven for an hour, or alternatively, let them dry in the sun.

In the meantime, prepare the seasoning by mixing the capers, anchovies, chillies/chiles and garlic together.

Take one half of the tomato and sprinkle with the seasoning mixture, then place the other half on top, kissing like a sandwich. Place the tomatoes on the bottom of a hot, sterilized jar one after the other until you reach the top. Cover with extra virgin olive oil, then seal and refrigerate. Enjoy in the winter.

# Caramelized red onion marmelade

3 tablespoons fruity extra virgin olive oil, plus extra for serving

3 red onions, chopped

2 bay leaves

a sprig of fresh rosemary, leaves picked

2 tablespoons balsamic vinegar

55 g/¼ cup packed soft brown sugar

**To serve**

4 slices of country bread, open textured, with a firm crust

4 handfuls of pea shoots

125 g/4½ oz. young Pecorino cheese

sea salt and freshly ground black pepper

SERVES 4

This recipe celebrates young Pecorino, which is gloriously sweet, and goes magnificently with the acidity of the onion marmalade. I enjoyed it at La Buca di San Petronio, a modern trattoria in central Bologna run by a young couple, Giorgio and Antonia Fini. I loved it, as well as the incredibly memorable pasta served with four wild herbs that followed.

Heat 2 tablespoons of the olive oil, then add the onions, bay leaves and rosemary. Brown the onions well over a low-to-medium heat, stirring regularly. Add the vinegar and stir well. Add the sugar and cook over a low heat for 30 minutes. The mixture should be thick, shiny and rich red. Leave to cool.

Heat a ridged cast-iron griddle/grill pan until hot. Add the bread slices and cook for 1–2 minutes on each side, until lightly toasted and charred at the edges. Put the pea shoots in a bowl, add the remaining tablespoon of olive oil and season to taste. Toss to combine.

To serve, spread 1 tablespoon of the red onion mixture on each piece of toast and put on serving plates. Add a handful of pea shoots and crumble the Pecorino on top. Sprinkle with more olive oil and pepper and serve.

# Pickled pumpkin

**1 medium pumpkin, weighing about 1 kg/2¼ lbs.**

**a generous pinch of fine sea salt**

**2 garlic cloves, blanched briefly in boiling water and roughly chopped**

**225 ml/1 cup extra virgin olive oil**

**50 ml/3 tablespoons white wine vinegar**

**2 teaspoons dried thyme**

MAKES 1 X 450-G/1-LB. JAR

I first encountered this delicacy in southern Italy. It is quite special and easy to make. Enjoy this pickled pumpkin in sandwiches and salads and as an accompaniment.

Using a sharp knife, cut the pumpkin in half and scoop out the seeds. Cut into sections, remove the peel and chop the flesh into small cubes.

Bring a large saucepan of salted water to the boil. Add the pumpkin flesh and boil for 4 minutes, until tender but firm (it should still have a little bite in it). Drain, put in a large bowl and leave to cool.

When cold, add the garlic to the pumpkin with the oil, vinegar and thyme. Mix well together, then pack in a hot, sterilized jar and cover. Store in a cool, dry, dark place.

# Pickled aubergines

**2 medium aubergines/eggplant**
**a few pinches of fine sea salt**
**2–3 teaspoons dried oregano**
**1 tablespoon white wine vinegar**
**2 garlic cloves**
**225 ml/1 cup extra virgin**
**olive oil**

MAKES 1 X 500-G/1-LB. 2-OZ. JAR

This is a Nonna Ferrigno recipe that makes a wonderful gift. It's utterly delicious with sourdough bread as a merenda (snack), or antipasto selection.

Slice the aubergines/eggplant into thin, short strips. Put in a colander and sprinkle with salt. Place a plate on top and weigh it down. Leave for 30 minutes to extract the bitter juices from the aubergine/eggplant.

Rinse the aubergine/eggplant well and put in a saucepan of boiling salted water. Boil for 4 minutes. Drain and leave to cool.

When cold, add all the remaining ingredients to the aubergine/eggplant and mix together.

Pack in a hot, sterilized jar and seal. Refrigerate and leave for a month before use.

# Piri piri marinade

**6 hot red fresh chillies/chiles, roughly chopped**

**2 teaspoons smoked paprika**

**4 garlic cloves, roughly chopped**

**freshly squeezed juice and grated zest of 1 lemon**

**½ cup/120 ml olive oil**

**sea salt and freshly ground black pepper**

YIELDS 130 ML/½ CUP

This is the perfect spicy condiment to enhance marinades, pastes and brines. Or even just drizzle a little on top of grilled vegetables.

Put the chillies/chiles, paprika, garlic, lemon zest and juice and olive oil in a food processor and process until smooth, then season with salt and pepper.

Store the piri piri in a glass jar in the fridge for up to 1 month.

Use piri piri as a wet rub to marinade meats before cooking, or as a condiment with meat, fish, poultry and vegetables.

# Japanese yakitori marinade

**3 teaspoons caster/granulated sugar**

**4 tablespoons soy sauce or tamari**

**4 tablespoons mirin rice wine**

**2 tablespoons sake**

**2 tablespoons groundnut oil**

Mix all the above ingredients together and use immediately.

# Matambre marinade

In Argentina they eat a lot of good beef, which is always seasoned before cooking. This simple marinade is perfect for steaks which can then be grilled or sautéd, as you prefer.

**1 teaspoon dried thyme**

**1 teaspoon dried oregano**

**1 teaspoon dried marjoram**

**1 teaspoon fine sea salt**

**½ teaspoon dried chilli/ red hot pepper flakes**

**2 garlic cloves, finely chopped**

**60 ml/¼ cup red wine vinegar**

**60 ml/¼ cup olive oil**

YIELDS 150 ML/ SCANT ¾ CUP

Put all the ingredients in a bowl and mix together.

Store the marinade in an airtight container in the fridge for up to 2 weeks.

To use, put the meat in a ceramic dish, pour over the marinade, and leave to marinate for 8–24 hours in the fridge. Let the meat come to room temperature, then cook as preferred.

# Korean marinade

This Korean-inspired marinade is one you will make over and over again and never tire of. Use it on pork ribs and fire up the grill! Or try it with lamb or even tofu for a tasty vegetarian BBQ option.

**80 ml/⅓ cup vegetable oil**

**80 ml/⅓ cup soy sauce**

**60 ml/¼ cup toasted sesame oil**

**3 tablespoons sherry**

**4 tablespoons brown sugar**

**3 tablespoons curry powder**

**2 tablespoons grated**

**fresh ginger**

**4 garlic cloves, peeled and bashed**

**3 spring onions/scallions roughly chopped**

**sea salt and cracked black pepper**

YIELDS 360 ML/ 1½ CUPS

Put all the ingredients except for the salt and pepper in a blender or food processor and process until blended, then season with salt and pepper.

Store the marinade in an airtight container in the fridge for up to 10 days.

To use, put the meat in a ceramic dish, pour over the marinade and leave to marinate for 8–24 hours in the fridge. Let the meat come to room temperature, then cook as preferred.

# French dressing

1 tablespoon Chardonnay white wine vinegar

1 teaspoon Dijon mustard

a pinch of caster/granulated sugar

4 tablespoons extra virgin olive oil

2 tablespoons sunflower oil

sea salt and freshly ground black pepper

MAKES 100 ML/ABOUT ⅓ CUP

Today the term French dressing is universal but originally it was used to describe a vinaigrette, which is an emulsion of oil and vinegar in varying quantities. To make a really good French dressing the balance of flavours should be just right – neither too sharp nor too oily. This recipe ticks all the boxes.

In a bowl stir together the vinegar, mustard, sugar, salt and pepper until smooth and then gradually whisk in the oils until amalgamated. Season to taste and serve.

Alternatively store in a screw top jar in the fridge for up to 1 week, shaking well before use. Use on any salad of your choice.

# Tarragon vinaigrette

2 teaspoons white wine vinegar or tarragon vinegar

1 teaspoon Dijon mustard

½–1 teaspoon caster/superfine sugar

2 tablespoons chopped fresh tarragon

3 tablespoons macadamia or hazelnut oil

1 tablespoon extra virgin olive oil

sea salt and freshly ground black pepper

MAKES 125 ML/½ CUP

When available, use macadamia nut oil in this dressing as it has a mild nutty flavour that really shows off the tarragon to its best. Hazelnut oil is also good and perhaps a more readily available alternative. If you really love the flavour of tarragon, use tarragon vinegar.

Place the vinegar, mustard, sugar, tarragon and a little salt and pepper in a blender and blend until combined, then add the oil and blend again until amalgamated. Adjust seasoning to taste and serve.

This dressing is delicious over a poached salmon salad.

# Walnut and vincotto dressing

1 tablespoon vincotto

2 teaspoons red wine vinegar

3 tablespoons walnut oil

1 tablespoon extra virgin olive oil

sea salt and freshly ground
black pepper

MAKES 75 ML/SCANT ⅓ CUP

Vincotto (cooked wine) is a sweet, dark syrup made from fermented grape must and comes from Apulia in the south of Italy. It is available from Italian delis and specialist food stores.

Whisk all the ingredients together, adjust seasoning to taste and serve.

Delicious drizzled over a tomato and rocket/arugula salad with shavings of aged Parmesan.

# Sherry, orange and raisin dressing

2 tablespoons extra virgin olive oil

30 g/1 oz. blanched whole hazelnuts

30 g/1 oz. raisins

3 tablespoons Pedro Ximenez,
sweet sherry or raisin juice

2 tablespoons sherry vinegar

grated zest and juice 1 orange,
about 3½ tablespoons

4 tablespoons hazelnut oil

sea salt and freshly ground
black pepper

MAKES 200 ML/1 SCANT CUP

Pedro Ximenez is an intensely sweet dessert sherry made from grapes grown throughout Spain. If unavailable, you could use Marsala or an alcohol-free alternative, such as raisin juice.

Heat the olive oil in a frying pan/skillet and gently fry the hazelnuts for 1–2 minute until golden, add the raisins and fry for a further 1 minute until soft.

Add the sherry and sherry vinegar to the pan and bubble for 30 seconds. Whisk in the orange zest and juice and warm through, then remove from the heat and transfer to a bowl. Gradually whisk in the hazelnut oil and season to taste.

Perfect served warm with a salad of duck, chicory/endive and orange segments.

# Sweet chilli dressing

75 ml/⅓ cup rice wine vinegar

50 g/¼ cup csaster/granulated sugar

2 red bird's eye chillies/chiles, thinly sliced

6 tablespoons peanut oil

freshly squeezed juice of ½ a lime

2 tablespoons Thai fish sauce

fine sea salt

MAKES 150 ML/⅔ CUP

Hot, sweet and sour together is a flavour combination we associate with Asian cuisine and this dressing epitomizes that. Using fresh bird's eye chillies/chiles will result in a fiery dressing so, if you prefer a milder heat, discard the seeds.

Place the vinegar, sugar and 1 tablespoon water in a small saucepan and heat gently to dissolve the sugar, then simmer for 5 minutes until the mixture is syrupy. Stir in the sliced chillies/chiles and allow to cool completely.

Whisk in the remaining ingredients until the dressing is amalgamated and adjust seasoning to taste.

This is wonderful drizzled over a Thai beef salad with tomatoes, cucumber, red onions and fresh herbs.

# Coriander and toasted sesame dressing

2 tablespoons sesame seeds

2 large spring onions/scallions, trimmed and chopped

1 tablespoon chopped coriander/cilantro leaves

1 teaspoon caster/superfine sugar

1 tablespoon rice wine vinegar

1 tablespoon light soy sauce

3 tablespoons sunflower oil

2 teaspoons sesame oil

sea salt and freshly ground black pepper

MAKES 150 ML/⅔ CUP

The toasted sesame seeds add a wonderfully nutty, smoky flavour to this Japanese-style dressing.

Dry fry the sesame seeds (without oil) in a small fry pan/skillet set over a medium heat until toasted and starting to release their aroma. Cool and transfer to a blender.

Blend to a paste with the spring onions/scallions, coriander/cilantro, sugar, vinegar, soy sauce and a pinch of salt. Add the oils and blend again until amalgamated. Adjust the seasoning to taste and serve. (Do give it a really good shake if you've prepared it ahead of time.)

Delicious enjoyed with any Asian-style noodle and vegetable salad.

# Wasabi, lemon and avocado oil dressing

**1 teaspoon wasabi paste**

**½ teaspoon caster/superfine sugar**

**1 tablespoon freshly squeezed lemon juice**

**3 tablespoons avocado oil**

**a pinch of fine sea salt**

MAKES 75 ML/⅓ CUP

Wasabi is Japanese horseradish, an integral ingredient in sushi and an accompaniment to sashimi. It adds a wonderful pungency to dishes and is lovely in a salad dressing. Rather than combining it with other traditional Japanese ingredients, here it is whisked with avocado oil and lemon juice for a refreshingly different flavour.

Place the wasabi paste, sugar, lemon juice and the salt in a bowl and, using a small balloon whisk, blend to form a smooth paste. Gradually whisk in the oil until amalgamated and adjust the seasoning to taste.

This is delicious drizzled over raw tuna or beef carpaccio or a cooked prawn/shrimp salad.

# Mirin dressing

**50 ml/3½ tablespoons mirin (Japanese rice wine)**

**1 spring onion/scallion, trimmed and thinly sliced**

**1 garlic clove, peeled and sliced**

**2 tablespoons rice wine vinegar**

**1 tablespoon dark soy sauce**

**2 tablespoons peanut or sunflower oil**

**1 tablespoon chopped fresh coriander/cilantro**

MAKES 150 ML/⅔ CUP

This is a mildly flavoured Japanese-style dressing with a little sweetness from the mirin, balanced beautifully with the rice wine vinegar. It is lovely served warm poured over oysters on the half shell or over grilled scallops.

Place the mirin, half the spring onion/scallion, the garlic, vinegar and soy sauce in a small saucepan. Bring to the boil and simmer gently for 2 minutes. Strain the liquid through a sieve/strainer and set aside to cool to slightly.

Whisk in the oil, stir in the chopped coriander/cilantro and remaining spring onion/scallion and serve immediately.

# Mexican lime, coriander and chipotle dressing

**1–2 teaspoons dried chipotle chilli/chile paste**

**grated zest and freshly squeezed juice 1 lime**

**1 teaspoon agave syrup**

**3 tablespoons pumpkin seed oil or avocado oil**

**1 tablespoon chopped fresh coriander/cilantro**

**sea salt and freshly ground black pepper**

MAKES 75 ML/⅓ CUP

Chipotle chillies/chiles have a wonderfully smoky flavour and aroma, giving this dressing a richness. You can buy dried chipotle chillies/chiles if you prefer but the paste, available from specialist food stores, is perfect for mixing into dressings. Both agave syrup and pumpkin seed oil will be available in health food stores.

Combine the chilli/chile paste, lime zest and juice, agave syrup and a little salt and pepper in a bowl and whisk until smooth. Gradually whisk in the oil until smooth, stir in the coriander/cilantro and serve.

Try drizzling this dressing over a shredded chicken, corn and avocado salad on a warm tortilla.


# Key West mango and lime dressing

**flesh of 1 small ripe mango, diced**

**grated zest and freshly squeezed juice 2 small limes**

**2 teaspoons clear runny honey**

**3 tablespoons avocado oil**

**1 red chilli/chile, deseeded and finely chopped**

**sea salt and freshly ground black pepper**

MAKES 150 ML/⅔ CUP

Mango flesh provides a great base for this pretty dressing, but you will need to buy a ripe mango. The dressing is perfect for serving with cooked prawns/shrimp and would make a great alternative sauce for the traditional prawn/shrimp cocktail with avocado and lettuce.

Place the mango in a blender with the lime zest, juice, honey and a little salt and pepper and blend until smooth, add the oil and blend again. Transfer to a bowl and stir in the chilli/chile. Adjust seasoning to taste and serve.

# Spiced Moroccan-style dressing

5 tablespoons argan oil

½ small onion, thinly sliced

1 garlic clove, crushed

1 teaspoon Ras al Hanout
(a Moroccan spice mix)

2 teaspoons pomegranate molasses

½ teaspoon clear runny honey

1 tablespoon finely sliced preserved
lemon

1 tablespoon red wine vinegar

sea salt and freshly ground
black pepper

MAKES 150 ML/⅔ CUP

This dressing uses Argan oil with a hot-sweet
Moroccan spice blend which can typically contain
a range of ingredients from ground coriander and
fenugreek through to kaffir lime and rose petals.

Heat 2 tablespoons of the oil in a small frying pan/skillet and
gently fry the onion, garlic, spice mix and a little salt and
pepper over a low heat for 5 minutes. Stir in the pomegranate
molasses and honey and warm through. Remove the pan from
the heat and whisk in the remaining oil. Stir in the preserved
lemon and adjust seasoning to taste.

Serve immediately. Try it poured over a chickpea salad with
shredded chicken, raisins, toasted almonds and freshly
coriander/cilantro and mint.

# Preserved lemon dressing

4 tablespoons extra virgin olive oil

1 tablespoon finely diced preserved
lemon

1 garlic clove, crushed

1 tablespoon freshly squeezed
lemon juice

2 teaspoons clear runny honey

1 tablespoon chopped fresh
coriander/cilantro

sea salt and freshly ground
black pepper

MAKES 150 ML/⅔ CUP

This salty-sour dressing with a hint of sweetness is
a real winner. Preserved lemons are now readily
available and can be found in larger supermarkets;
alternatively try Middle Eastern food stores and delis.

Combine all the ingredients in a blender and blend until
smooth and vibrant green.

Drizzle over a salad of couscous, shredded grilled/broiled
chicken, tomatoes and fresh spring onions/scallions.

# BAKING AND SWEET THINGS

## My traditional carrot cake

200 g/1⅔ cups Italian
'00' flour

½ teaspoon fine sea salt

1½ teaspoons baking
powder

¼ teaspoon bicarbonate
of soda/baking soda

½ teaspoon ground
cinnamon

¼ teaspoon ground
cloves

¼ teaspoon freshly
grated nutmeg

250 ml/1 cup sunflower,
or grapeseed oil

250 g/1¼ cups packed
brown sugar

3 UK large/US extra
large eggs, lightly
beaten

zest of 1 unwaxed
organic orange

2 teaspoons pure vanilla
extract

80 g/⅔ cup lightly
toasted fresh walnuts,
chopped

175 g/1⅔ cups (about
3 medium) carrots,
coarsely grated

30 g/⅓ cup desiccated
coconut

FOR THE FROSTING:

200 g/1 scant cup cream
cheese

95 g/7 tablespoons
unsalted butter,
softened

1½ tablespoons maple
syrup

finely grated zest of
1 unwaxed organic
orange

50 g/⅓ cup icing/
confectioners' sugar

fresh walnut halves,
to decorate

a 24-cm/9½-in.
loose-based cake pan,
greased and lined

SERVES 6–8

When I ran my own restaurant, this
cake was made for us by a lifelong
vegetarian lady who was rather severe
in appearance, but gentle and shy. This
was her cousin's recipe. Her cakes were
demolished by our customers, one man
making a round trip of 65 km just for
a slice!

Preheat the oven to 170°C (325°F) Gas 3.

Sift the flour, salt, baking powder, bicarbonate of
soda/baking soda and spices into a mixing bowl.

Combine the oil, sugar and eggs in a separate
small bowl.

Add the orange zest, vanilla extract, walnuts,
carrots and coconut to the flour mixture. Add
the oil and egg mixture and stir well to combine.
Spoon the cake batter into the prepared cake
pan and level the surface. Bake in the preheated
oven for 1 hour until a metal skewer inserted
into the centre of the cake comes out clean. Let
cool in the pan for 5 minutes and then turn out.

For the frosting, beat the cream cheese with the
softened butter, maple syrup, orange zest and
icing/confectioners' sugar. Spread on top of the
cool ake, and decorate with a few walnut halves.

# Antonia's award-winning chocolate fudge cake

Feather-light, rich, chocolatey and award-winning. My little girl's great baking success!

175 g/1⅓ cups Italian 'oo' flour

2 tablespoons finest-quality unsweetened cocoa powder

1 teaspoon bicarbonate of soda/ baking soda

2 teaspoons baking powder

140 g/¾ cup light brown sugar

2 tablespoons golden/light corn syrup

2 UK large/US extra large eggs

150 ml/⅔ cup organic sunflower oil

150 ml/⅔ cup buttermilk

2 teaspoons pure vanilla extract

100 g/3½ oz. dark/bittersweet chocolate, drops or chunks

**FOR THE FROSTING:**

100 g/7 tablespoons unsalted butter, at room temperature

180 g/1¼ cups icing/confectioners' sugar

3 tablespoons finest-quality unsweetened cocoa powder

a drop of whole milk

freeze-dried strawberry pieces, to decorate (optional)

two 18-cm/7-in. cake pans, greased and lined

SERVES 6–8

Preheat the oven to 180°C (350°F) Gas 4.

Sift the flour, cocoa, bicarbonate of soda/baking soda and baking powder into a mixing bowl. Add the sugar and stir to combine.

Make a well in the centre of the flour mixture and add the syrup, eggs, oil, buttermilk and vanilla extract. Beat with a hand-held electric mixer until smooth.

Spoon the mixture into the prepared cake pans and bake in the preheated oven for 25–30 minutes until a skewer inserted into the centre of the cake comes out clean. Let cool in the pans before turning out onto a wire rack to cool completely.

Melt the chocolate in a heatproof bowl set over a saucepan of gently simmering water. Do not allow the base of the bowl to touch the hot water. Spoon the melted chocolate onto a piece of baking parchment and allow to set. When the chocolate has set, use the back of a knife to make curls with the chocolate to scatter over the top of the cake.

To make the frosting, put the softened butter in a bowl and beat, gradually sifting in the icing/confectioners' sugar and cocoa and adding the milk to make a fluffy, spreadable buttercream.

Sandwich the cooled cake with half of the frosting, using the remaining half to cover the top and the sides. Use a palette knife to apply it and smooth it over the cake to cover.

Scatter the chocolate curls and strawberry pieces (if using) on top.

# Italian almond apple cake

Born out of a glut of apples, this is the happy result of an experiment.

200 ml/¾ cup olive oil

225 g/1 cup plus 2 tablespoons light brown sugar

3 UK large/US extra-large eggs

225 g/1¾ cups Italian 'oo' flour

1 teaspoon ground cinnamon

2½ teaspoons baking powder

½ teaspoon cream of tartar

600 g/1¼ lbs. tart dessert apples, peeled, cored and diced

100 g/⅔ cup raisins

75 g/¾ cup flaked/slivered almonds

finely grated zest of 2 organic unwaxed lemons

a 20-cm/8-in. springform cake pan, greased and lined

SERVES 6–8

Preheat the oven to 180°C (350°F) Gas 4.

Pour the olive oil into a mixing bowl. Add the sugar and beat until smooth with a hand-held electric mixer.

Add the eggs, one at a time, and beat until the mixture has increased in volume and resembles a thin mayonnaise.

Sift together the flour, cinnamon, baking powder and cream of tartar. Add these dry ingredients gradually to the oil mixture, folding them in with a metal spoon.

Add the apples, raisins, flaked/slivered almonds and lemon zest. Spoon the mixture into the prepared cake pan and bake in the preheated oven for 1 hour until a skewer inserted into the centre of the cake comes out clean.

Let cool slightly in the pan before turning out onto a wire rack to cool completely before slicing to serve.

# The ultimate banana bread

Oil creates a winning texture in cakes – I hope the following recipe will convince you! I have had a lifetime's passion for bananas and a corresponding lifelong pursuit of the best banana recipes.

**100 g/⅔ cup dried dates**

**240 g/2 cups Italian 'oo' flour**

**50 g/½ cup porridge/old-fashioned rolled oats**

**3 teaspoons baking powder**

**50 g/½ cup chopped pecans**

**1 teaspoon fine sea salt**

**60 g/⅓ cup soft brown sugar**

**120 ml/½ cup sunflower oil**

**200 g/¾ cup Greek yogurt**

**75 ml/⅓ cup coconut milk**

**5 UK large/US extra-large eggs**

**60 g/¼ cup clear runny honey**

**2 teaspoons pure vanilla extract**

**225 g/1 cup mashed bananas, super ripe (i.e. black)**

a 30-x 17-cm/12-x 6½-in. loaf pan, greased and base-lined

SERVES 12

Preheat the oven to 180°C (350°F) Gas 4.

Soak the dates in boiling water for about 12 minutes.

Put the flour, oats, baking powder, pecans, salt and sugar in a mixing bowl and stir to combine. Mix the sunflower oil, yogurt, milk, eggs, honey and vanilla extract in a separate bowl or jug/pitcher.

Drain the dates, remove the stones/pits and chop finely. Add the bananas and dates to the wet ingredients. Pour the wet ingredients into the dry and mix together until combined.

Spoon the mixture into the prepared pan and bake in the preheated oven for 40 minutes until golden and a skewer inserted into the centre of the cake comes out clean.

Let cool slightly in the pan before turning out onto a wire rack to cool completely before slicing to serve.

45 g/⅓ cup polenta/fine cornmeal

200 g/1 cup golden caster/raw cane sugar

100 g/1 scant cup ground almonds

1½ teaspoons baking powder

215 ml/1 scant cup olive oil

4 eggs, lightly beaten

finely grated zest of 1 unwaxed organic orange

finely grated zest of 1 unwaxed organic lemon

2 tablespoons icing/confectioners' sugar

FOR THE SYRUP:

45 g/3½ tablespoons granulated sugar

freshly squeezed juice of ½ an orange

freshly squeezed juice of ½ a lemon

1 cinnamon stick

a 21-cm/8-in. cake pan, greased and lined

SERVES 8

# Tunisian cake

This particular cake is an all-time family favourite, and has always been received well. I love the fact that it can all be mixed together in one bowl.

Combine the polenta/cornmeal, sugar, almonds and baking powder in a mixing bowl.

Using a wooden spoon, beat in the oil, eggs and the orange and lemon zest. Pour the mixture into the prepared cake pan and put into a cold oven. Turn the oven on at 190°C (375°F) Gas 5 and bake the cake for 35–40 minutes. Remove from the oven, let cool for 5 minutes, then turn out onto a wire rack.

Meanwhile make the syrup. Simmer the sugar and juices with the cinnamon stick for 5 minutes, stirring to dissolve the sugar, then remove and discard the cinnamon stick.

Prick the cake all over with a skewer and pour the syrup over the cake while it is cooling. Serve dusted with the icing/confectioners' sugar.

# Lemon, lime and cardamom crisp crackers

I'm a passionate breadmaker and these wonderfully crispy crackers are the result of a happy experiment. The lemon and lime zest are a perfect partner to the cardamom. I like to serve these crackers with ice cream or soft fruit as the crunch of the crackers counterbalances their velvety texture. A sprinkle of icing/confectioners' sugar gives them a lovely finish.

**15 g/½ oz. fresh yeast or 7 g/¼ oz. dried/active dry yeast**

**250 g/9 oz. strong white unbleached flour, plus extra for sprinkling**

**½ teaspoon fine sea salt**

**50 ml/3 tablespoons coconut oil, plus extra to stretch and roll the dough**

**finely grated zest of 1 unwaxed organic lemon**

**finely grated zest of 1 organic unwaxed lime**

**2 teaspoons ground cardamom or 8 cardamom pods finely ground in a mortar with a pestle**

**125 g/⅔ cup white caster/ granulated sugar**

**TO SERVE:**

**icing/confectioners' sugar**

**two oiled baking sheets**

MAKES 12–16

Measure 50 ml/3 tablespoons warm water in a jug/measuring cup. Blend the fresh or dried/active dry yeast with a little of this water.

Sift the flour and salt together into a mixing bowl. Make a well in the centre and add the coconut oil, along with half the lemon, lime, cardamom and sugar mix, the yeast liquid and some of the water. Mix together with a wooden spoon, gradually adding the remaining water, to form a soft dough.

Turn the dough out onto a lightly floured work surface and knead vigorously for 10 minutes until it is soft and satin-like (don't be afraid to add more flour). Place in a lightly oiled large bowl, then turn the dough around to coat with the oil. Cover the bowl with a clean kitchen towel and leave in a warm place for 1½ hours, or until the dough has doubled in size.

Preheat the oven to 200°C (400°F) Gas 6. Place the prepared baking sheets in the bottom of the oven.

Knock down the dough with your knuckles, then turn onto a lightly floured work surface and knead for 2–3 minutes to knock out the air bubbles. Divide the dough in half.

On a lightly floured work surface, preferably marble, roll out the pieces of dough very, very thinly, until 25–30 cm/10–12 in. in diameter. Now lift each cracker onto a cold baking sheet and top with the remaining half of the lemon, lime, cardamom and sugar mix.

Carefully slide the prepared crackers off the cold trays directly onto the hot baking sheets and immediately bake in the oven for 12 minutes until golden and crisp. Dust with the icing/confectioners' sugar. When cold, crack them and enjoy!

# Baked figs with hazelnuts and balsamic vinegar

Italy's best figs come from the Naples area, having had all summer to ripen in the hot sun. Frangelico goes beautifully with figs, but you could use a sweet vermouth instead.

**12 ripe fresh figs**

**115 g/1 scant cup of shelled hazelnuts, toasted and halved**

**1 tablespoon mild clear runny honey**

**2 tablespoons good balsamic vinegar**

**3 tablespoons Frangelico (hazelnut liqueur) or sweet red vermouth**

**115 g/½ cup fromage frais**

SERVES 4

Preheat the oven to 200°C (400°F) Gas 6.

Cut a tiny slice off the bottom of each fig so that it will sit stably. Make two cuts down through their tops, about 2.5 cm/ 1 in. deep, at right angles to one another. Ease each fig open, squeezing their middles to make the 'petals' open.

Mix most of the nuts with the honey, balsamic vinegar, Frangelico and fromage frais. Spoon this into the opened-out figs and arrange them in a baking dish. Bake in the preheated oven for 15 minutes until the fromage frais is bubbling. Sprinkle over the remaining toasted hazelnuts and serve.

# Olive oil ice cream

This original recipe comes from Giovanni Fassi at the Palazzo del Freddo in Rome. It will be devoured by even the fiercest sceptic. Serve with chocolate balsamic vinegar (see page 32).

**200 ml/¾ cup whole milk, or coconut milk for a dairy-free option**

**140 g /¾ cup golden caster/raw cane sugar**

**100 ml/½ cup double/heavy cream**

**5 UK large/US extra-large egg yolks**

**160 ml/⅔ cup fruity olive oil**

an ice cream maker (optional)

SERVES 4–6

Put the milk, sugar and cream in a saucepan and slowly bring to the boil over a medium heat. Stir to make sure the sugar has dissolved. Remove from the heat and leave to cool.

Whisk the egg yolks in a bowl with a balloon whisk.

When the milk and cream mixture is cool, add the egg yolks, a little at a time, to the pan over a low heat. You are aiming to create a custard. When the egg and milk mixture has thickened enough to coat the back of a spoon, remove it from the heat. Add the oil and whisk the mixture with a balloon whisk until well incorporated.

Transfer the mixture to the ice cream maker and churn according to the manufacturer's instructions. Alternatively, pour it into a metal tin in the freezer. You will need to remove the tin from the freezer and whisk the ice cream vigorously every hour and a half until it is set and smooth.

# Dessert cocktails

Vinegar-based cocktails are currently a favourite on the London cocktail circuit and rightly so. The vinegar cuts through the sweetness of the cocktail, adding a delicious sweet and sour flavour. You'll have difficulty stopping at one glass!

## Queen of tarts

A balsamic strawberry temptress.

**6 fresh strawberries, puréed**
**3 teaspoons caster/granulated sugar**
**30 ml/1 oz. dry martini**
**15 ml/½ oz. vodka**
**freshly squeezed juice of ½ a lemon**
**3 teaspoons good balsamic vinegar**

SERVES 1

Muddle the strawberries with the sugar in a cocktail shaker. Add the martini, vodka, lemon juice and vinegar. Add ice cubes and shake until chilled. Strain into a cocktail glass filled with ice to serve.

## Mon chéri

For all those chocolate and cherry lovers!

**30 ml/1 oz. Grand Marnier (or other orange-flavoured liqueur)**
**15 ml/½ oz. white rum**
**2 tablespoons finely grated dark/ bittersweet chocolate**
**5 ml/¼ oz. part maraschino (cherry) liqueur**
**2 teaspoons cider vinegar**

SERVES 1

Fill a cocktail shaker with ice. Add all of the ingredients and shake until chilled. Strain into a cocktail glass filled with ice to serve.

# Index

# Acknowledgments

Without their culinary insight and input this book could not have been written. I love working as a team and this has all been possible with the expert guidance and assurances and support from:

Julia Charles, Nathan Joyce, Leslie Harrington, Toni Kay, Jan Baldwin, Emma Marsden, Charles Carey, Frances Jaine, Anne Dolamore, Judy Ridgway, Juliet and Peter Kindersley, and Eric Treuille. Also to Sally Daniels for her utterly professional approach, speed, efficiency and the ability to decipher my scribbles. Thank you.

# Picture credits

Food photography by:
**Jan Baldwin** Pages 1–4, 6–9, 13–17, 22–23, 27–140
**Ian Wallace** Pages 5, 19, 20

Travel photography by:
Page 11 © Thomas Hoepker/Magnum Photos
Page 24 nimu1956/istockphoto

# About the author

Ursula Ferrigno is an acclaimed and experienced food writer and chef who embodies the Italian and Mediterranean passion for good food made from the freshest natural ingredients. She trained at the Auguste Escoffier School of the Culinary Arts and has herself taught at leading cookery schools in both the UK and Italy, including the celebrated Leith's School of Food and Wine, Divertimenti and La Cucina Caldesi in Ireland. She toured the United States, running classes in Sur la Table stores, is consultant chef to the popular Caffè Nero restaurant chain and has made numerous appearances on BBC television. The author of more than 17 cookery books, Ursula has also written for numerous magazines and other publications, including *Olive* and *BBC Good Food* magazines, the *Observer*, *Taste Italia* and *American Gourmet*.